SUPPORTING ARSENAL 101 (Row 25)

David Fox

SUPPORTING ARSENAL 101 (Row 25)

DAVID FOX PUBLISHING

Copyright © 2024 David Fox

All rights reserved. No part of this book may be reproduced or used in any manner without the prior permission of the copyright owner.

To request permissions, contact the publisher at
info@davidfoxpublishing.com

eBook: ISBN 978-1-0686363-0-1

Paperback: ISBN 978-1-0686363-1-8

Cover art by Ruth Beck (www.ruthbeckart.com)

Cover design by David Fox & Norbert Dudkiewicz

The views and opinions expressed in this book are those of the author and are not necessarily representative of Arsenal Football Club.

DAVID FOX PUBLISHING

www.davidfoxpublishing.com

For Michael

Table of Contents

There's a book in everyone _____ 1
Becoming an Arsenal Supporter _____ 5
   A Father's tale _____ 7
   A Son's tale _____ 11
Being an Arsenal Supporter _____ 15
   True Supporter? _____ 17
   Match Day routine _____ 20
The 2023/24 Season _____ 23
   A trophy won! _____ 25
   The Premier League is back in N5 _____ 28
   Dominant, but not clinical enough _____ 30
   Rollercoaster of emotions _____ 32
   False start but a happy ending _____ 34
   The times they are a changing _____ 37
   Back in the UCL, and I missed it! _____ 39
   Should've won, could've lost _____ 41
   The invisible game _____ 43
   Really missing live football _____ 44
   Another lead slips away _____ 45
   One nil to the Arsenal! _____ 47
   Rice inspires comeback _____ 50
   Growing in Europe _____ 52
   View from The Avenell Club _____ 54
   Not good enough _____ 56

Fuming!	57
It wasn't supposed to be this easy!	59
We will remember them	61
A very Happy Birthday!	64
Europe take note	65
Missed opportunities didn't cost us	67
Declan Rice you beauty!	69
Missed opportunities cost us this time	71
Changes made, same quality shines through	72
Football and Family	74
We are definitely title contenders!	77
How did we not score?!	79
WTF was that performance?!	81
"We need a killer"	83
We're back!	86
Deja vu!	89
Back in the title race!	91
Really respectful Rice	94
Who needs a new striker?	96
Reality check	98
Back in the groove	100
Record breakers	102
Kai Havertz scores again!	104
A very tense and very late night	107
A point won, or a missed opportunity?	111
Low key rise to the top	113

Back on top (for now) in style	115
No bad teams at this stage	117
Emery's revenge	121
Running out of steam!	124
Superb on the road	126
On cloud nine (literally)	128
Derby Day Delight	130
Taking it to the wire!	132
They think it's all over, but not yet!	135
It wasn't to be	138
Continuing to be an Arsenal Supporter	141
Where does the team go from here?	143
What's next for the Fox boys?	145
Glossary of terms	147
About the author	148

There's a book in everyone

I'd been going over the Arsenal for forty nine years before I finally became the proud owner of a season ticket.

From September 1972, through the "boring" football of the seventies, the Charlie Nicholas haircut of the early eighties, the George Graham years of success then mediocrity, the Arsene revolution, the "Invincibles", a Champions League final, the move to the new stadium, the lean years while we paid for it, the resurgent FA Cup wins, the farewell to Arsene, the Emery debacle to the rebirth under Arteta. The club changed dramatically and I grew from a seven year old, watching with his Dad and Brother, to a fifty something Dad sitting with his grown up son.

It was my son, Michael, who pushed for us to get the season tickets, though I didn't need much encouragement. We were only actually on the waiting list proper for eight years before we were elevated to the coveted Gold Membership, I gather the wait now is over fifteen years! In the three seasons since we have seen performances that range from the incredibly frustrating to the amazingly brilliant. Games that left us feeling every emotion from misery to elation, anger to ecstasy. Football does that to you and Arsenal has, over the years, been the master of delivering the most extreme of emotions.

I've always loved going to the Arsenal but these last few seasons have given me the opportunity to spend more time with Michael, doing something we both love. It's not all sweetness and light, we certainly have our moments where we argue and annoy each other. What father and son don't? But the joy of celebrating a late winner against a fierce football rival is intensified when we are able to share it together. In those moments of unbridled joy, I realise how lucky I am, not just to be there at the game, but to be there with my son. I really do love the big lump!

The last game of the 2022/23 season was a 5-0 thumping of Wolves. As I left the stadium that day, I realised the following season could be my last full one. We have no plans to give up the season tickets but a likely house move will make travelling to home games more difficult.

So, I had the idea of capturing the 2023/24 season in a book and dedicating it to Michael. I've always enjoyed writing and have wanted to write a book for years but never seemed able to find the time, motivation or subject to write about. "Write about what you know" they say. Well Arsenal fits that bill. There was a contestant on Mastermind once who chose Arsenal as his specialist subject. I got every question correct, with no passes, so I reckon that qualifies me.

My "writing process" consisted of making mental and written notes during, and shortly after, games and then expanding them as soon as I could. I make no apology for omitting opposition team players' names or referring to them, or their teams, by a different name/term. These are my accounts of the games, intended for fellow Arsenal supporters. Other fans are very welcome to read this book, and I hope they enjoy it, but I naturally have, and bring, an Arsenal perspective. If some of the specific details about matches, goals, stats, etc are incorrect I can only say they are what I genuinely believed to be true at the time. When you are in a stadium and get just one look at an incident, you often get the wrong impression or mix up players. If that doesn't make the case for VAR I don't know what does. We just need VAR to be run by competent individuals with proper training in the technology. More on that later.

My original plan was to just include accounts of the matches we actually attended but, on reflection, felt that would leave too many holes in the story of the season. So, I have included all the away games and the small number of home games I wasn't able to get to (my bad, full explanations follow). Generally, the account of the games I watched on tv are shorter, though there are a few exceptions where something happened that riled me enough to want to vent some frustration, e.g. Newcastle away!

After the first game, the Community Shield victory, I realised that my views and memories of the day, changed after watching highlights, reading reports and listening to podcasts. As I want the book to capture what we experienced in the moment, I separated the account of each game in to the immediate raw, emotional and often slightly drunk view and then a Next Day View (NDV). The NDV is usually much more considered and rational. Usually.

Once I had the collection of match reports written I felt the book needed a bit more depth about me and Michael; how we got in to football, what does supporting the club mean and what does a trip to the stadium involve? All that has been added and, hopefully, you will find it enhances the story.

We pay a lot of money for our season tickets but we love going to the Arsenal and are immensely proud of what the club represents. There is a class about the way things are done, there always has been. To see some of the money we spend donated by the club to so many worthwhile causes, through the Arsenal Foundation, is heart warming. I'm all too aware that we, as season ticket holders, are in a privileged position that most are not, and that many would love to be.

My primary reason for writing this book was to be able to present it to Michael as a memory and keepsake, that's why it's dedicated to him. Of course, I hope it achieves some level of commercial success but that genuinely is not my main motivation. And as my way of giving something back for all the enjoyment the club gives us, I am donating a percentage of my author royalties to the Arsenal Foundation. I hope the knowledge that some of the money you paid for this book will go to help those who really need it will add to your enjoyment.

Come On You Gunners!

Becoming an Arsenal Supporter

A Father's tale

Most people can tell you all about the first football match they attended but I'm not entirely sure about mine. I have always believed it was a 2-1 win against Chelsea at Highbury but, having researched it, the game played in September 1972 ended in a 1-1 draw. I'm sure it must have been that one though.

I'm guessing now, but I suspect the reason I was finally allowed to go to a match was partly because of a major disappointment a few months earlier. In May 1972 Arsenal made it to the FA Cup Final to play Leeds. Some of my Dad's family were from Yorkshire and his Uncle Jack worked on the ground staff at Elland Road. The night before the Final about twenty rough and ready Yorkshire blokes turned up on our doorstep asking to crash for the night. My Mum was less than pleased but reluctantly agreed. Uncle Jack had two spare tickets so my Dad and older brother, Simon, went to Wembley. I wanted to go but was told I was too young, probably code for there wasn't a ticket for me. It turned out to be a blessing in disguise as the tickets were in the middle of the Leeds fans. Arsenal lost 1-0 and my poor brother, decked out in red and white standing out like a sore thumb, cried his eyes out.

If the Chelsea game wasn't my first (which the more I think about it the more convinced I am that it was) I do know I was definitely at the game against Liverpool, also in September 1972. That is quite a famous match as it's the one where the linesman was injured and Jimmy Hill, the famous ex player and pundit, came down from the tv gantry to run the line in his place. I remember his light blue tracksuit as he charged up and down in front of us. We were sat in the West Stand for this, and the Chelsea, game. Now, of course, that stand is an apartment block. Enjoying the luxury of a seat was not normal in my early years, I suspect my Dad decided that taking two small boys to a game warranted paying the extra to avoid the crush of the Clock End terrace.

To be honest, I was more interested in watching the marching Metropolitan Police Band at half time than the actual football, but the experiences fired up something in me and I've loved watching and playing football ever since. Full disclosure: I did dabble with supporting other teams in those, early, formative years. Superstar players drew my interest, Osgood at Chelsea, Stan Bowles at QPR, Keegan at Liverpool, but I always liked the Arsenal and was always destined to be an Arsenal fan.

We played football on the council estate where we lived every chance we got. As the youngest I was always shoved in goal but actually became half decent from all the practice I got. The wisdom of diving around on the clay tiled "pitch" is debateable, my jeans would be caked in dust and smell peculiar after several hours of playing. First team to score 20, change ends at 10. We had to play to get our football fix because we couldn't afford to go to matches very often and there were only three games live on the tv every year - the FA Cup Final, the European Cup Final and the England v Scotland Home International.

After those first couple of games we migrated to the Clock End for our occasional visits to Highbury, standing at the very back so us boys could perch on the safety railing while holding on to Dad. Then my Mum and Nan pulled off a masterstroke. They would sell "Useless Eustace" tickets, a kind of lottery come scratch card thing where you won prizes based on a cartoon caption in the Daily Mirror. Not particularly mind blowing in their own right but the seller got a free ticket to the Clock End for the home games. So for a season or two in the mid seventies we could go to every game. Well, almost every game. Man Utd, Tottenham, Leeds, Chelsea, West Ham and Liverpool were all off limits due to the extra large crowds and likely fighting that would take place. Even so, we went to loads of games and I gradually got more interested in the actual football, though would be distracted by the cheap peanuts on sale by the bloke wandering the terraces. It's hard to shell peanuts and watch Alan Ball's white boots at the same time. I remember one match v Burnley which I think ended 0-0. It absolutely poured with rain the whole game so we stood at the front under my Mum's see through umbrella, a very popular seventies accessory.

After the free tickets stopped (I suspect Mum and Nan couldn't sell enough and couldn't afford to buy them all themselves) I would go to "combination" (reserve) games at Highbury. Games drew a crowd of a few hundred but the whole stadium was open so you could sit or stand wherever you liked. I was broadly interested in watching the football, most of which wasn't very good, but as a ten year old the opportunity to mess about with my mates often got the better of me. We were threatened with ejection several times by the stewards, though they never actually followed through with the threat.

Through secondary school I went to every game I could. The first European night was brilliant - unfortunately not good enough to remember who we played. The best bit was it was my first time in the North Bank. I loved it. The singing was nonstop, it was loud, we got pushed around all over the terrace as the crowd swayed. It's that I remember rather than what happened on the pitch.

When I started work I used my wages for two things - beer and Arsenal. I'd meet up with school mates, Paul and Jeff, in the Marquis Tavern in Canonbury then we would walk to the ground. Paying £3 to get in, we would head to the bar at the back of the North Bank, get two beers each then take up our regular positions. I went to every home game in the 1983/4 season (plus a few away) and only missed Chelsea and Liverpool at the start of the 1984/5 season. I was in Ibiza for the Chelsea game and my brother married his wife, Shan, on the day we played Liverpool. Bad planning on all our parts. That's a theme we will develop later.

When I first started going out with Mary she was also a regular at Highbury. She lived within earshot of the ground and would go with her brother, Teague. After we got married we moved to Essex and could no longer afford to go to games that often. The mortgage interest rate was 12% after all. Games were few and far between for a number of years but I always watched on tv and managed to get tickets for the 1987 League Cup Final. We stood at the very back of the Arsenal end at Wembley, miles from the pitch, but an incredible atmosphere as we won the cup against Liverpool.

My daughter, Nicola, and son, Michael, were always destined to become Arsenal fans. I did sit them down when they were about four or five and told them they could support any team they wanted but, if they decided it wasn't to be Arsenal, they would need to let me know where they were moving to. Boomer parenting of the finest order.

When Arsenal moved to the Emirates I had an option on two season tickets but Michael was playing in a Youth Football team which I managed; I didn't do any coaching as such, that was down to my good friend Kev (Chelsea fan!). I promised Michael we would get season tickets if, and when, he stopped playing. The team stayed together for ten seasons so we finally joined the waiting list in 2013, it took until 2021 to finally get the tickets!

A Son's tale

I know exactly which game was Michael's first, 5th March 2002, an evening game v Derby. We won 1-0 on our way to winning the Premier League title. Like my first game, it was at Highbury and we had seats, but the ground had changed a lot in the three decades that had passed. Jeff got us seats in the front row of the North Bank, just to the side of the goal.

In the warm up Thierry Henry shot just wide and the ball rebounded off the fence and hit Michael. He wasn't so much hurt as shocked but I consoled him by saying "I've been coming over here for thirty years and never touched the ball, you've not been here thirty minutes and you have!". It sort of worked. These days, we would probably get Henry's shirt and a social media post for that.

In the first half Arsenal dominated and all the play was up our end. This helped to keep Michael's interest, though he did keep telling me the time - "Daddy, we've played thirty five minutes". "Daddy, we've played thirty seven minutes now", " Daddy, we've played thirty eight minutes now". You get the picture. When Thierry attempted an overhead kick that went just over Michael shouted "I can do that!". Several people around us looked at him and nodded approvingly. What he actually meant was that he could make Thierry do that on his Play Station.

Pires scored the winning goal at the Clock End so we couldn't see it very well but Michael can say he was there when we won a game in the title winning season. I should have taken a more careful note of the view from the front, see the upcoming chapter on the Community Shield for an explanation. He enjoyed the experience but I think being allowed to stay up late and getting a hot dog (yes he got ketchup all over his coat) were as much a part of it as the football.

We managed to get tickets for a game in the final season at Highbury. Nicola joined us and we sat in the old West Stand Family Enclosure. It really didn't work very well due to the design of the stand. Everyone would stand up whenever we came close to Bolton's goal, at that point the kids had to stand on their seats to have any chance of seeing the pitch. It was a drab game, we drew 1-1 with a Gilberto Silva goal.

We struggled to get tickets for the Emirates at first, demand was unsurprisingly high. Our first game was against Newcastle. We were poor and Newcastle led for a large part of the game. But Thierry stepped up and curled a free kick in to the top corner to earn us a point. After, as Michael's football playing career took up all weekend, we mainly went to League Cup games and even Portugal v Brazil just to get a chance to go to the stadium. Even so, Michael has retained his love of the Arsenal and relishes every chance to go to a game. In more recent years (just prior to getting the season tickets) we got to Europa League and FA Cup games but could never get tickets for the biggest matches. As Red members it was difficult, I gather that situation is even worse now with the Ticket Ballot scheme.

We expected to only have to wait for a couple of years to get the season tickets once we had joined the waiting list, the team hadn't had much success and people were not apparently renewing at a high rate. Then with the FA Cup wins in 2014, 2015 and 2017 interest clearly picked up again delaying our advance to the top of the list until 2021.

To fill the void left by not playing/managing the Youth Team anymore we decided to tour Europe for some top class football. Weekends away to Dortmund, Bayern Munich, PSG, Ajax, AC Milan, Barcelona, Anderlecht (Brussels), Benfica, PSV Eindhoven and Real Madrid were all brilliant experiences and certainly brought the two of us closer together. Beer does that! But it was big games at the Arsenal that we really craved.

Then in 2021 the offer of season tickets finally came. I have to say it was a torturous process, some poor chap having to manage it all over the phone. There were several options available but we wanted the North Bank upper tier and that's what we got.

At last we had reached the Holy Grail - two tickets for every home game, right in amongst the passionate Arsenal fans. With hindsight, we underestimated the actual commitment required to attend all the games. The rest of your social life has to take a bit of a back seat and arranging family events becomes very difficult, but we both feel it's worth it. I wavered a bit after the first year, unsure if another season was worth the financial cost and family impact. Michael convinced me to renew and I'm so glad I did because, in the last two seasons, Arteta has inspired the club to challenge the very best, and the football and stadium atmosphere are absolutely fantastic.

Being an Arsenal Supporter

True Supporter?

What is a "True Supporter"?

I've seen much online debate (argument) about this. To me, the idea that you are only a true supporter if you go to every game, home and away, and haven't missed one for forty years is absolute nonsense. If you go to every game, home and away, you are definitely a supporter and clearly very loyal. But consider the commitment required by those that live, say, on the West Coast of the USA or in India or Australia. They will have to get up early or go to bed late just to watch us play. Imagine watching a match at 3am on a Monday morning before having to go to work.

There are thousands of fans who would love to be able to go to every game but simply cannot, due to location, money or other commitments. They still get the same pleasure and delight from seeing Arsenal win. They still feel upset, annoyed and even angry when we lose.

I think the True Supporter is one who feels that emotion - good and bad - and has a personal connection to the club. And no two people will have exactly the same connection, that's why it's personal. I've gone through phases of attending lots of games in a season, periods where I couldn't afford to go at all, times when I could afford it but couldn't get a ticket for love nor money. Throughout all of this I watched games on tv when I couldn't go, read the newspaper reports and, in more recent years, trawled social media for information and video of the matches. When we won I was happy, when we lost I was sad. So, yes I consider myself a true supporter and that didn't change just because I couldn't get to the stadium.

Those who are able and willing to devote so much of their life and money to going to games, and are in a fortunate position to be able to get tickets for home and away matches, deserve immense credit for their dedication. Their support, financial and physically cheering the team on, is critical. Arteta has referenced the need for fans to help the team if the club is to be successful on the pitch, so we absolutely need those supporters there every week.

What about booing the team, or calling for the manager to be sacked? I did both in the eighties, calling for Terry Neil to resign or be sacked after an awful run. I stood outside the main entrance after a game chanting "sack Terry Neill", though that wasn't quite as severe as the bloke next to me dressed in a vicar's outfit shouting for him to jump from the boardroom window and promising to provide salvation. I don't know if he was a genuine vicar but, either way, that was perhaps a step too far.

I was more "Wenger In" than "Wenger Out" but felt his time had come to an end. I wanted him to leave after the FA Cup Final win over Chelsea, to go out on a positive note with his head held high. But I also felt he had earned the right to decide when he should step down; he gave so much to the club and changed not only Arsenal, but the entire face of English football with his methods and approach to the game. I know many people felt different, and that's fine. I think, as a supporter, you are entitled to your opinion and have the right to voice your views, as long as it doesn't cross the line in to abuse, which it seems to be doing more and more unfortunately. You pay your money (ticket, Sky subscription, etc), you get to choose how you feel and how you express it.

When I heard our fans singing "you're not fit to wear the shirt" to our players, in an away match at Crystal Palace a few years ago, I felt deeply uncomfortable. It felt too harsh to me but I wasn't there and hadn't spent time and money travelling to away games to watch a team that appeared to have given up. So, while I probably wouldn't have sung that, I respect the right of those that did. I don't feel that crossed a line, it felt like it was true supporters voicing their concerns, having reached the end of their tether.

I doubt this chapter has changed many people's views on what constitutes a True Supporter. That wasn't my aim, I just wanted to stimulate the debate by putting forward my own personal view. I'll conclude by saying that I consider myself to be a True Supporter who also happens to be lucky enough, and privileged enough, to be able to afford a season ticket at the Emirates and have the time, and understanding family and friends, that enables me to go to the games.

Match Day routine

I'm a creature of habit, actually scratch that. I'm a control freak with a severe touch of OCD. That manifests itself on match days as needing to follow a similar routine and check every detail required to ensure the day runs smoothly. Of course, it often doesn't, but it's not for the want of planning. Michael just kind of turns up and watches a game of football. He must take after his mother. Actually, he's a carbon copy of Mary's brother in so many ways. I can live with that.

My preparation for match day begins a day or two before with the first crucial decision: train or drive? My preference is to use the trains (it takes three to get there) and have a couple of beers but, for midweek games, that means getting home very late. Then at weekends C2C (our local train operator) and TFL often decide to thwart my plans by undertaking maintenance work. Driving is easier but is also prone to traffic problems on the notorious A13. Then there is the issue of parking. We park about twenty minutes walk from the ground so, ultimately, driving and public transport take about the same amount of time door to door. So, generally, it's drive in the week, trains at the weekends unless they are completely screwed up.

Having prepared travel plans and actually got to the stadium, the next step is gaining entry. We try to get in early as there have been a few issues with the entry system that has caused long delays and there's nothing worse than being stuck in a queue for the turnstile knowing the game has started. After the search by the security team, I hold my breath that the digital pass will work and the gate will illuminate a comforting green to denote I've passed the test and can enter. To be fair to the club, most issues seem to have been resolved but you still see a few people stunned as the gate illuminates red and denies entry.

Once in you are confronted by the lower concourse. For big games, or when an earlier kick off is being screened, this area is packed with people. Often the singing is in full swing as people are getting in the mood for our game. It's nice if a rival game is showing and they are losing as we can all cheer their misery.

I make my way up the stairs to the upper concourse. I've never counted the steps, surprising from an OCD stand point, but usually get to the top a little out of breath despite being relatively fit for my age. Now the next big decision point. Do I need to use the toilet? At this stage there probably isn't a queue and, as I've probably been in a car/train for almost two hours, it makes sense to. Let's move on quickly.

Food and/or a drink are next up. The quality of the food is a bit hit and miss. When it's good it is very nice and (almost) worth the considerable price. When it's bad it's really bad. I always complete the fan surveys when invited by the club, and always highlight the need to improve the food quality and consistency. I'll be more positive about the beer, especially as it's half price for a period before each game. The switch to Camden Hells was, according to Ray Parlour, the best transfer Arsenal made a couple of summers ago. I do my best to support this decision whenever I'm not driving.

We usually meet on the upper concourse as Michael often travels to the ground separately. Once we are ready to take our seats we enter Block 101 and I always turn right and loop round to the stairs up to row 25. That's a superstitious thing as we lost a game when I turned left once. I like to be in my seat, or more to the point standing at it, before the teams emerge from the tunnel. "London's Calling" by the Clash is played and then the current video and accompanying music is shown on the big screen prior to the teams being introduced. I cheer every Arsenal player as their name is read out. As the team gather for their huddle "The Angel" is played. I love that song (very well done Mr Louis Dunford), it is perfect for this club, so I sing along heartily.

Then kick off and the real fun starts.

At half time I usually stay where I am, Michael will often disappear for food or to meet his mate, Charlie, for a beer. I cannot get any proper mobile (cell phone for the USA folks) signal and wifi is nonexistent so I usually just watch the kids taking penalties against the eight foot dinosaur, Gunnersaurus.

At the end of the game we always stay to the bitter end. I understand why people leave early but really wish so many wouldn't. It can kill the atmosphere. We applaud the team off, win, lose or draw. We don't leave until the last of them, usually Martin Ødegaard, leaves the pitch. Then it's a quick pit stop at the toilet before the journey home. If we are on the train we will often grab a beer on the lower concourse to let the queues at the station subside. Better to be sipping a beer than queuing outside a station I always feel.

There are a few slight variations to the above, especially for UEFA Champions League games, but this will give you a fair insight. I imagine most people have some sort of regular routine, it goes back to everyone experiencing football in their own way. So, now you know what our "normal" match day looks like, let me take you through each match of the 2023/24 season as experienced by us, being Arsenal Supporters.

The 2023/24 Season

A trophy won!

Sunday 6th August 2023
FA Community Shield Man City (n) 1-1 (4-1 on pens)

Whether you view the Community Shield as a pre season friendly, a chance to set down a marker against a rival or a full blown trophy (like Jose Mourinho does) it has been the season curtain raiser for as long as I can remember and definitely not a game you want to lose. Perhaps it's fair to say most supporters dismiss it if they lose but enjoy it if successful.

I haven't been to one before and after last season's amazing progress, despite the fizzling out at the end, expectations for this season are high in the Fox household. I'm not saying we are going to win the league but I fully expect us to be in contention all the way, Michael is his usual bullish self and has declared we will win not just the league but the Champions League as well. Oh the optimism that comes with youth!

I got three tickets as soon as they went on sale, Charlie is joining us for what is planned to be a bit of a session prior to kick off. We meet Charlie at the station and I'm immediately surprised by the number of football shirts on show. Not just Arsenal but some team from Middlesex (they didn't become North London until 1965 when the GLC was formed and boundaries changed - Google it). I hadn't realised they have a meaningless friendly today while we have a mighty clash for an important trophy at Wembley!

A quick pit stop for a coffee at Liverpool Street, as it's still quite early, then we jump on the tube and head for Wembley Park. We have lunch booked near the stadium, including bottomless cocktails. Could get messy.

After filling our boots we stroll round to the Arsenal side of the ground, there's no animosity among rival fans, most people are just enjoying the sunshine and the fact the football is back, but there is something comforting about strolling by the Arsenal fan zone and just seeing a sea of red shirts, with the odd fake away ones on show despite the club not actually selling them yet!

We decide to get in to the ground as soon as possible to avoid any issues that may arise, it's Wembley after all. A couple of beers on the concourse, songs breaking out among the ever growing crowd of Gooners, then we take our seats. Actually we didn't sit down, not at any point in the day. Michael had insisted we get seats near the front behind the goal. I gave in and now regret it completely. The view of the pitch is poor, it's difficult to determine positions of players and as everyone else is standing we have to do the same despite only being in row three.

I'm not going to give a blow by blow account of the game as, frankly, I don't remember much through the pina colada and beer haze that has engulfed me, but I do remember thinking Rice was everywhere, Timber looks excellent and that Palmer kid for City looks a prospect. His goal looked to have ruined the day but there was a sense among the crowd, and more importantly among the team, that we don't give up that easily. A deflected shot from Trossard right in front of us in the eleventh minute of injury time takes us to penalties.

As it becomes clear the penalties are at our end suddenly the view seems ok. Michael is quick to point this out after all my moaning. I'm nervous. "It's only a friendly" I tell myself. It's not! We really want this. Not just because winning is always nicer than losing. Not just to make the long journey home a bit better. This really is a chance to show we are getting closer to City. They are the team to beat, beat them and it will give the team and the fans more confidence.

Ødegaard scores, De Bruyne hits the bar, Trossard slots home, Silva does the same, Saka scuffs one in to the corner, Rambo saves from Rodri. Up steps Vieira and sticks it in the top corner. The whole end of the ground erupts, we leap on each other, I'm hugging Michael and jumping up and down. We've won!

The players run to Rambo and Vieira in the corner, the coaches and subs charge on, the noise is deafening and the relief palpable. The other end starts to empty, they're in the shade while the Gooners celebrate in the bright sunshine, it's as poetic as it is sublime. We stay behind for ages, singing and cheering as the trophy is presented and paraded.

Eventually we make our way home, standing in line for the underground station for the best part of an hour, more singing, all very happy Gooners. Much nicer when you win!

NDV: Seen a lot of nonsense about us over celebrating, honestly why are people so ridiculously down beat on everything. I watched the highlights when I got home and, as the replay of Vieira's penalty is shown from the camera behind him, there we are! All three of us, poised ready to explode with joy. The ball hits the net, there's a split second of silence, then up we go. Then a big club flag is raised obscuring us. Still, we got on the telly.

The stats demonstrate it was a close game. Were we closer to being ready for the season than them? Probably. Did we ride our luck with the two great stops from Ramsdale? Definitely. Were we lucky with the deflection for the goal? Absolutely. Will the result have any tangible impact on our team and their confidence? Possibly. Is it a proper trophy that we are glad to have won? You bet your bloody life it is!

The Premier League is back in N5

Saturday 12th August 2023
Nottingham Forest (h) 2-1

After the "cup final" feel of last weekend's Community Shield, we are back on more familiar territory for the early kick off at the Emirates to start the league campaign. It's Michael's birthday so we grab a late breakfast and early beers in the ground. The sun is shining, there's a buzz around the concourse at block 101. It's great to be back among Arsenal fans at home, there's something special about the club these days, a feeling of being back among friends after not seeing them for ages. Add to that the expectation of a strong season, having hopefully learned and grown from the disappointing end to last season just a few short months ago.

Forrest don't look like they are going to offer much, everyone is confident of a win to start the league campaign. Conversations about the score all favour Arsenal, 3-1, 4-0, 5-0. My own prediction is a 2-0 win.

We climb the steps to our seats, nodding hello to the familiar faces of fellow season ticket holders that sit around us. It's all smiles, so great to be back. The players emerge to a huge cheer and applause. For those that were unable to get to Wembley last week it's their chance to let the players know how much the win was appreciated. For me, and the thousands who were at Wembley, another chance to shout their names and relive those memorable minutes after last week's trophy presentation. The Angel is sung with extra feeling by everyone, absolutely including me and the big fella next to me (Michael obviously). I feel really excited and emotional. Blimey we've got months of this in front of us!

Forrest don't appear to have read the script, they break through one on one with Ramsdale but thankfully the striker blasts way over. Phew!

It seems to liven us up. Martinelli shows a bit of trickery to beat two defenders and Eddie fires home to put us ahead on 26 minutes. Shortly after, Saka scores a trademark goal, beating three defenders and curling the ball into the top corner for 2-0. There's obvious delight with both goals but it's more a feeling of being satisfied we have met expectations than the outpouring of emotion a late winning goal brings.

To be honest, the beer kicks in and most of the rest of the game has already faded from my memory. We seemed to pass it around comfortably and create the odd chance but as a contest it felt long over. Our quiet Saturday afternoon is suddenly punctured when Timber goes down without a challenge and is withdrawn. My first reaction is that it seemed similar to when Robert Pires picked up his knee injury all those years ago. "Don't say that!" the bloke next to me says (not Michael). Fingers crossed it isn't serious as he looks a top class player already.

The injury definitely puts a dampener on the atmosphere and then Forrest add a big slice of jeopardy when they grab a late goal. What was a stroll in the park now feels like a real uphill battle but we hold on and take the three points.

A few more beers to celebrate and then I make my way home with Charlie's dad, Gary, and his mate Jason, while Michael heads off with Charlie to continue his birthday celebration.

NDV: Timber's injury is an ACL, my first feeling was right unfortunately. Looks like he'll miss most, if not all, of the season. A terrible shame for him, a big blow for the squad but we have to deal with it. City won comfortably and already have a better goal difference than us. It's going to be a long season and we are going to have to close games out better than we did with this one if we are to mount a challenge to them.

Dominant, but not clinical enough

Monday 21st August 2023
Crystal Palace (a) 0-1

Away to Palace is never an easy game, especially under the lights. Michael rarely watches games on tv with me unless it's a real big one so I settled down to watch it on my own, expecting a difficult game but one I felt we would ultimately triumph in.

In the first half we exerted control and created some great chances. Eddie missed two glorious opportunities; I just don't think he's at the level we need. Saka put a great chance wide and Ødegaard drew a good save from the keeper.

Our dominance continued in the second half and, when Eddie won us the penalty and then Ødegaard tucked it in the corner, I expected us to go on and win easily. But step forward the referee, apparently desperate to be part of the story. Ayew slipped past Tomi and when Tomi breathed on him he threw himself to the ground. It wasn't even a foul in my opinion, definitely not a yellow card. Tomi was already on a yellow for being in the wrong place at the wrong time. He had stepped up to take a throw when the referee lost patience over perceived time wasting, mainly because the crowd were complaining. You expect a bit of common sense to prevail, give Tomi a talking to with the captain as a final warning (that's part of the FA escalating protocol which few commentators seem to know about) then get on with the game 11v11. No, let's send him off. Ridiculous.

We then had to play out the match under the cosh, thankfully this team is much more solid than previous iterations and we saw it through.

NDV: The more I see of that sending off the worse it feels. But to be honest it shouldn't have mattered. We should have been out of sight by half time. If there's one thing we need to add, to what looks like a phenomenally strong defence, it's clinical finishing. I'm just not sure we have the players we need for that yet. Still time to buy before the window shuts.

Rollercoaster of emotions

Saturday 26th August 2023
Fulham (h) 2-2

It's a lovely sunny, early season day at the Emirates and a rare 3pm Saturday kick off. Even the trains are working so we arrive in good time to find the upper concourse at block 101 tingling with anticipation after the win at Palace. The beers are flowing nicely and Michael and I are enjoying a pre match chat about tactics and selections.

Whenever I have doubts about renewing our season tickets, and there have been a couple of times where I did have some, it's days like this I think of to make me see sense. Precious memories of just chilling out at the stadium, a beer in hand and talking mostly bollocks but without a care in the world. And it's these memories that seem to linger longer these days. I love watching the football but, to be honest, I struggle to remember games now after a few days, though still have vivid memories of games from years ago: 3-2 win at Highbury against that lot, Charlie Nicholas scored the winner and I was in the photo on the back of the News of the World next day, for example. I guess the vast majority of games bear little significance in their own right, though can form an important part of what sometimes becomes a successful and memorable season or cup campaign. Perhaps that's why they slip from the memory so easily, or is it just because I'm getting old. I'll let you, the reader, decide. Michael has already ventured his opinion. It's because I'm an old bastard apparently.

We take our seats and join in with the singing of The Angel, I suspect I'm even more loud and off key than usual due to Camden Town Breweries' finest! The game kicks off and, oh no! Saka gives the ball away and Fulham score a well taken long shot that finds Rambo way out of position. It's like last season all over again. Another defensive lapse sees Fulham come close to doubling their lead. The crowd are losing patience, there's an anxiousness all around me. I've got a horrible feeling about this one.

Things improve in the second half and Vieira wins a penalty. Up steps Saka, I'm nervous. He's not. He sends the keeper the wrong way and rushes to recover the ball. 1-1 game on. Almost immediately we are back on the attack, Vieira crosses and Eddie gets on the end to side foot home. We all go mad, jumping and screaming. 2-1 and the mood has completely changed.

When the Fulham defender fouls Eddie to prevent a break and picks up his second yellow card it all feels like game over. Unfortunately not.

Fulham score from a late corner, the attacker finding space to shoot despite the fact that every Arsenal player is in the penalty area. Arrrgh!

The mood in the ground changes again. It feels like a defeat despite picking up a point. We make our way home in a decidedly less celebratory mood than we had hoped for.

NDV: Arteta said he felt we should have scored a hat full of goals. Whilst I agree it does raise the question of striking ability. I really don't think Eddie is at the level we need, despite his well taken goal in this game. If we are going to have a chance to win the title we need to be clinical and put games to bed. City demand you have to be almost perfect to finish above them. We are just not at their level in front of goal, even if you exclude the Norwegian robot. Still a couple of days left for Mikel to open the cheque book. Does anyone even have a cheque book anymore?

False start but a happy ending

Sunday 3rd September 2023
Man Utd (h) 3-1

As a kid I wasn't allowed to go to Man Utd games because in the 70s there was always a lot of fighting. This is always a big game, regardless of how good or bad both teams are playing. I'm in confident mood though as they really do look a shadow of their former selves and, even if our last outing was disappointing, you sense Arteta will have the team fired up.

I took a nice stroll to the train station in glorious sunshine with the intention of having a few beers after the game with Michael. But C2C, ever mindful of my liver, decide to cancel the train. The next one gets me to the Emirates about fifteen minutes after kick off. Great. A quick call to Mary to pick me up and, once I drop her back home, I'm on the A13 with everything crossed. Luckily, the roads are clear and I arrive just in time, but no time to stop for any refreshments so it's straight up to my seat where Michael is waiting.

We look good from the start without creating too much. Utd are sitting deep and clearly looking to hit us on the break, which they do with a well taken goal from Rashford. I felt Ramsdale could have done better at the time, he got a hand to it, but after seeing the replays maybe that's a bit harsh. Rashford celebrating in front of us drew a few shouts of "poor show old chap" or words to that effect.

We didn't take the blow lying down, striking back within a minute. A slick passing move down the left, Martinelli picks out Ødegaard and he smashes it home for 1-1 at half time. Great strike, it seems we always score that exact same goal against Utd.

When Havertz squeezes past two defenders and is brought down 60,000 voices cry "penalty". The ref agrees. VAR doesn't and it's overturned. This is where VAR needs work for those who have paid to be in the ground. You wait for ages, don't get to see any replays and then are expected to just accept the decision. Nice idea if they didn't have such a poor track record of getting it wrong!

As the second half a plays out it feels more and more like the next goal will win the match. With three minutes remaining Utd break the offside trap and score. I don't believe this. We have been the better side but again look like dropping points in a game we should win. And then VAR to the rescue. They didn't break the offside trap. It must've been very close.

A late corner finds Declan Rice unmarked at the far post, he chests it down and blasts it. It takes a deflection but flies in to the corner right in front of us. Everyone is on their feet, the screams are phenomenal and we are all jumping over each other. I grab Michael, always a good thing to do at times like this because it stops me from falling on the bloke in front. The ground has gone mad, except for one corner in the Clock End lower tier which is a sea of calm in the early evening sunshine.

Declan has just established himself as a fan favourite. £100m? Worth every penny.

But we're not finished yet. Vieira sets Jesus away with a perfect pass on the half way line. Jesus carries it confidently in to the area, fakes to shoot, waits for the sliding defender to get out of the way and tucks the ball in the far corner for a memorable goal that absolutely seals the victory. I love goals like that, the crowd all stand up when he's put through, a hush descends, a murmur of expectation as he sets up his strike then an eruption of noise as the ball hits the back of the net.

We stay to applaud every last Arsenal player off the pitch, Declan gets a special cheer. Then we head home where a cold beer and a late dinner await.

My old mate Steve, proper Manc fan from Oldham though he lives in the USA now, sent me a very simple text at full time. It read "fuck off!". I'll take that all day long.

NDV: Ten Hag spent the entire evening disputing their offside goal. Apparently the lines were wrong. The stats show we were the better team on the day, they only managed two shots on target. We left it late but got the result, but it was another very emotional end to the game and last season that seemed to wear the team down. Hopefully we can start to control games better and get the job done earlier, if only for the sake of my blood pressure. There's a few teams bunched at the top of the table as you would expect at this early stage, annoyingly there's an international break now so we have to listen to that lot down the road going on about how they are above us for at least a fortnight.

The times they are a changing

Sunday 17th September 2023
Everton (a) 0-1

We don't usually do well at Goodison and, although I've never been to the ground, I'll be glad to see the back of it when they move out to their new stadium. We need to win this one to start to create some momentum to our title challenge. The three points against United was great but we have got to start controlling games better, and not rely on late goals and emotional moments to win games. We found last season that wasn't sustainable, as much as I hate to admit it the pundits were right about that.

I'm at home watching on tv, the first half was pretty uneventful apart from what, at first, looked a great goal from Martinelli. VAR checked and declared it offside unfortunately. Gary Neville questioned the camera angle used for the decision, it did look a bit suspect and not what you would call conclusive. Cue Twitter/X conspiracy theory posts.

Ødegaard brings a save out of the keeper early in the second half and we are pushing for the goal. A one touch passing move is finished brilliantly by Trossard and we have our lead. You expect an onslaught from Everton from that point, driven on by their vociferous support, but we have a defence that is rapidly maturing and starting to bring comparisons with previous generations. We keep our shape well and deny them chances.

In fact, we should have doubled the lead from a breakaway but again the keeper saved from Ødegaard and Vieira's follow up was well blocked.

So a good win in the North West. We were overdue one.

NDV: A dominant performance all over the pitch. We restricted Everton to just one shot on target and 26% possession. There's a long way to go, and I'm not sure Everton is much of a benchmark for the rest of the league, but it's great to come away from this with maximum points and sets us up for the UCL which starts on Wednesday. Unfortunately, I'm off on holiday and will miss it! Better not let Mary hear me say "unfortunately"!

Back in the UCL, and I missed it!

Wednesday 20th September 2023
UCL PSV (h) 4-0

OK I messed up. In January we booked a holiday to Corfu and I gambled that we would either be away for the first UCL group game or that we would play on the Tuesday. Of course the draw puts us at home on the Wednesday, the first night of our holiday.

But a true football fan always finds a way and there I was, after a very good pre match meal in one of the hotel restaurants, propped up at the bar to watch the Arsenal announce themselves to the rest of Europe.

It took us just seven minutes to find the breakthrough, who else but Saka to score it? Ødegaard's shot was saved by the keeper but the star boy followed up and fired home with his right foot.

After that we just ran riot. Trossard with a great strike from the edge of the box made it 2-0, Jesus brought a fine save out of the keeper and then, a few minutes later, found his scoring touch with a thunderbolt from close range for 3-0 at half time.

The game was won by this stage but we kept pushing for a fourth, and it finally came with twenty minutes to go. Ødegaard with a perfectly placed shot from outside the area in to the corner, giving the keeper no chance.

As the game wore on, and the beers kept pouring, I swapped texts with friends and family at home. I don't think any of us expected it to be this easy. At the end of the game I felt a few pangs of regret for missing the first UCL game at the Emirates for seven years, but I consoled myself with the fact I didn't have to wind my way home through heavy London traffic or on a packed train. The salted caramel espresso martini helped as well.

NDV: I spent much of the day on a sun bed by the pool, drinking pina coladas while watching highlights and trawling social media for videos posted by fans at the game. Still annoyed I missed it but at least my seat wasn't empty as one of Michael's mates went in my place. The general feeling is that this was a top class performance but there is a long way to go, and there will be much more difficult tests ahead.

Should've won, could've lost

Sunday 24th September 2023
Tottenham (h) 2-2

My pre match routine for this one consisted of lying on a sun bed drinking cocktails and eating club sandwiches as the Corfu holiday continues. As much as I'm disappointed about missing the UCL game, missing this match is an even bigger regret. The North London Derby at home is the first fixture I look for when the league programme is announced. Mary's brother Teague, a lifelong and very passionate Arsenal fan, always made sure he got a ticket for this game. Then he would stand right next to the away fans and enjoy the "friendly banter" that always ensued.

I've passed my ticket to today's game on to a friend of Michael's to ensure the seat isn't empty and Michael confirmed the atmosphere was every bit as good as you would expect.

The hotel didn't have the game on tv so I had to go old school and listen on the radio! It was like being back in the 70s, but nowadays you are able to watch replays of the goals on social media within a few seconds so I kept up with the action pretty well.

A deflected Saka shot opened the scoring, it's a shame it didn't go in the top corner, where it was headed before hitting the defender, as that would have been an all time classic derby goal.

Then Jesus missed a great chance to double our lead, firing way over the bar. With hindsight that was a critical moment. I'm convinced that if that had gone in we would've won comfortably. But it didn't and it seemed to give Spurs belief. Raya made a great save when it looked for all the world that they had equalised. He had no chance though when poor defending allowed them to pull the ball back from the touch line and for Son to score off the post.

We were awarded a penalty after a VAR check, I don't think they can have any argument but I'm sure they will. Saka stroked it in to the middle of the goal and I thought we would go on to win from there. Unfortunately, an uncharacteristic error from Jorginho let them in for an equaliser within a minute of the restart. They had a dominant spell after that, we definitely missed Rice who had gone off injured at the break. In the end I was happy to take the point but we have to do better at holding on to leads, especially at home in big games. As Michael summed the game up in his text to me that evening, "should've won, could've lost".

NDV: More social media trawling on a sun bed but my impression from yesterday remains. Disappointed we didn't hold on to the lead, twice. Thankful that we held on to a point in the end. Gutted to have missed it all despite the idyllic nature of the holiday destination.

The invisible game

Wednesday 27th September 2023
EFL Cup Brentford (a) 0-1

Not a lot to say about this game as it wasn't shown on tv in the UK, or anywhere else as far as I can see. I watched brief highlights which suggests it was all Arsenal though the stats didn't bear that out. It was an opportunity for Arteta to play a few of the squad players and rest some of the bigger names, something Arsene Wenger used this competition for to good effect over the years.

For the goal, Brentford gave the ball away to Eddie, he pulled it back to Reiss Nelson who tucked it away well. Apart from that, the Brentford fans gave Ramsdale some expected grief and that's about all I gleaned from what little I was able to see. We won, we move on to the next round.

NDV: I'm not sure if the squad players did enough to earn a start in the next fixture, Eddie's goal is probably the stand out action. Not much more to add really. Seems odd the EFL haven't come up with a plan to allow these games to be streamed. They must be missing out on some sorely needed revenue.

Really missing live football

Saturday 30th September 2023
Bournemouth (a) 0-4

A 3pm Saturday kick off is great when we're at home but really frustrating if we're away, as we were for this one.

I'm not in to the dodgy streaming lark so have to keep up with the game via Sky Sports. It's an odd concept, watching an ex player watching a game and telling you what's going on. Then you have to fill in the missing pictures via Match of the Day. It's almost like being back in the 70s, or Corfu!

Saka put us in front with a rare headed goal, the keeper stranded after Jesus headed against the post. Eddie won a penalty which Ødegaard put in the corner, sending the keeper the wrong way. Ødegaard was fouled for our second spot kick which was gifted to Havertz to open his Arsenal account. Ben White headed in from a free kick to round off the day. Real shame I couldn't watch this live.

NDV: A lot of nonsense on line about how the Havertz goal was a sympathetic gesture, adding to the opposition fan narrative that he was a waste of money. Arsenal fans have come up with an ironic song about that and I spent ages watching YouTube videos of our fans singing and dancing along to it. Comfortable win, tougher challenges ahead no doubt.

Another lead slips away

Tuesday 3rd October 2023
UCL Lens (a) 2-1

I was expecting this to be a tough game but one that I felt we should win. When Jesus put us in front within fifteen minutes I was convinced we would take the points and top the group. But, similar to us, Lens have been out of this competition for a while and their fans were in high spirits and making lots of noise. It definitely helped give them belief they could get back in to the game, and then Raya's wayward pass gifted them the ball and the chance they needed. That said, there was a lot to do once they got the ball and the final shot was a superb finish but, once again, we have given up a lead when we were looking reasonably comfortable. That's a trend we have to stop if we are to have any success this season.

Both teams had chances in the second half but it was Lens who finally took one with twenty minutes to go. We huffed and puffed in front of goal but couldn't find the finish to equalise. Disappointing result, something isn't quite there yet, we play well in patches and are scoring goals but aren't yet controlling games for the full ninety minutes. This isn't a terminal blow but we are going to need to improve on this performance if we are to get out of the group.

NDV: With PSV and Sevilla drawing we are still top of the group so no real damage done with this result. Hopefully this young squad, many of whom are playing in the UCL for the first time, will learn from this. I do feel that experience counts for a lot in this competition and that you have to learn how to win it over a few seasons. Next game in this group is a difficult away game in Sevilla. But our next fixture is the small matter of City at the Emirates.

One nil to the Arsenal!

Sunday 8th October 2023
Man City (h) 1-0

Big game today, we need to get something out of it. A win would be brilliant because we haven't beaten them since 2015 in the league, as the various media outlets keep reminding us, but I'd take a point just to keep them in touching distance. Obviously, after only seven games, this is no title decider. But you can see City being as strong in the run in as they were last season, and having to make up any sort of gap will make a title challenge very difficult.

Michael heads off to London early for a pre game gym session while I go through my own pre match ritual - two sausage and egg muffins and a couple of episodes of the Whitehouse and Mortimer Gone Fishing programme to calm my nerves.

With an NFL game in another north London stadium, TFL are advising train and tube congestion so I take the strategic decision to drive up. Turns out to have its own issues as the Blackwall Tunnel is closed, great planning people!

No major drama ensues though and I get to the ground in time, grab a £5 Pepsi and make my way up to our seats. Michael is elsewhere in the ground with his mates, replacing the calories he burned earlier with a few pints.

The ground looks full in time for a rousing rendition of The Angel and there's a definite nervousness mixed with anticipation in the crowd. David

Raya does nothing to build our confidence with a couple of early mishaps and somehow we conspire to turn his possession into a City corner. They almost score, Declan Rice heading off the line, an early sign of the top class performance he's about to put in. Nathan Ake blasts over after a flick on sees him clear seven yards out. An early sign of his unfortunate day perhaps.

After a shaky and nervous fifteen or twenty minutes things settle down, and that's just me! We get on the front foot a bit but Eddie isn't showing much up front. "He needs to do more" I say, before he takes a through ball, turns inside and shoots wide. Probably should have hit the target but he's got in the game. "I just don't think he has enough of a presence" I say to Michael just before Eddie chases a City player and makes a crunching slide tackle on half way to force the ball out. The whole stadium erupts, the temperature and atmosphere rising. "You were saying?" Michael asks with a "you know nothing Jon Snow" vibe. I'm part way through re-watching Game of Thrones.

I'm not going to dwell on the two Kovatic fouls, he should have probably been sent off for the first on Martin Ødegaard, he should definitely have gone for the second one on Rice. Obviously Michael Oliver felt these were not as bad as the heinous offences Martinelli committed that night he sent him off for blocking a throw and pulling back a player in a ten second spell. Ridiculous.

Half time and Michael nips off to refresh himself further while I stand and try to get something out of WhatsApp, never easy as reception is poor. The first half stats surprise me a little - 5 shots to 3 in our favour.

Martinelli on for Trossard who we later learn was injured, which probably explains his poor performance. We look better immediately and have the better of the first fifteen minutes. That said it still feels very tight, I wouldn't be surprised if it ends 0-0 and can't see more than one goal, and no idea which team will get it. Pep makes substitutions, "who?" I sarcastically shout as the incoming players are announced. With the talent he's bringing on it's even more tongue in cheek than usual. Arteta responds (to Pep's changes, not my shouting) with Partey, Tomiyasu and Havertz. Please let this be Kai's day. And it sort of is. Now we have a threat up front, helped by Tomiyasu playing as a striker from left back! Five minutes to go, Partey sends it long. Tomiyasu nods it down to Havertz who isn't able to get a shot off, but does well to hold it up before laying it perfectly into Martinelli for a first time shot. The shot is on target though would probably not have troubled the keeper, but a ricochet off Ake's face wrong foots him and it's a goal. The place goes crazy. It's Bournemouth all over again but times ten. Everyone is jumping up and down, the noise is phenomenal and I'm hugging Michael. I actually kissed him in the Bournemouth celebration but the lack of beer clearly makes me more restrained today.

We all sing "1-0 to the Arsenal" and it's never sounded so good or tasted so sweet. We control the four minutes of injury time like, well, like City normally do and there's another explosion of noise and emotion at the final whistle. The stadium DJ plays The Angel again (master stroke) and the still very full stadium belts out "North London Forever" as my voice starts to croak. Amazing atmosphere, so much for the Highbury Library. We have the much coveted win and leap frog City in the table, for now at least. This feels like a massive psychological boost for our young squad but time will tell if it is genuinely a turning point.

We make our way back to the car and home with a celebratory beer in The Duchess of York at Michael's insistence. Rude not to.

NDV: Turns out this was the lowest number of shots City have had under Pep, just four and only one on target. Saliba's stats are incredible, what a player! This was a real statement win which should give everyone, players and fans alike, the confidence that we can be successful.

Rice inspires comeback

Saturday 21st October 2023
Chelsea (a) 2-2

I really fancy us to win this one as Chelsea are not in great form and the win over City, before the international break, has boosted our confidence no end. I settle down in front of the tv with a lovely stein of Oktoberfest beer in expectation of an enjoyable evening. It doesn't last long.

I don't think you can really argue about the penalty, it's accidental but, nowadays, a raised arm in the area is usually going to result in a spot kick. We were looking a bit ragged, where's the calm confident team from a couple of weeks ago gone? They almost get a second and I'm hoping Arteta can sort things at half time.

Before we get a chance to see, they are two up. A poor cross from Mudryk drops in at the far post. Total fluke, it had to be him didn't it? Raya is rattled and presents a golden opportunity for a third before making amends. This is horrible to watch.

Then a lifeline. The keeper makes a poor clearance and Rice hits it first time from distance right in the corner. We're inside the last fifteen minutes. Game on.

Talk about momentum change, it's now all Arsenal. Chelsea are rattled now and Saka picks out a perfect cross for Trossard to volley home. Suddenly, my living room is alive to the sound of drunken cheers. Side note: I do tend to drink quickly when I'm nervous. We almost win it late on but Eddie turns his (difficult) shot wide. I'm possibly being unfair but I think a top class striker, which is definitely what we need, scores that. We have to settle for a draw but it actually feels like a win. Time for another beer in that case. Hic!

NDV: Some nonsense from Mudryk claiming he meant the goal is best ignored. The performance deserves a bit more scrutiny. The game turned on the Rice goal. We need to make what happened after that the norm, not the exception.

Growing in Europe

Tuesday 24th October 2023
UCL Sevilla (a) 1-2

Sevilla have a very good record in Europe, albeit more in the Europa League/UEFA Cup than the UCL, and at home they are usually strong and difficult to beat. So, with this potentially the most difficult game in the group stage, I sat down to watch prepared to take a point. Obviously Arteta and the team were not.

We looked in good form from the start, taking the game to Sevilla and creating chances. But it took until first half injury time to make the breakthrough.

A high clearance was taken down with ease by Jesus midway in our half. He then turned two defenders and set Martinelli away with a perfect pass in to his stride. Martinelli out ran the chasing defenders, steadied himself, rounded the keeper and slotted home for 1-0. A truly magnificent goal.

I anticipated a surge in pressure from Sevilla at the start of the second half but it was Arsenal who came out strong. We had two good chances to extend the lead within five minutes but White and Ødegaard both fired over the bar. Then Jesus collected the ball wide on the left. He cut inside and curled a ferocious shot in to the top corner for 2-0. I took a celebratory sip of my water - yes water, I don't actually drink that much/often despite what you may have read prior to this!

Sevilla pulled one back with a bullet header from a corner and then brought an outstanding save out of Raya. His finger tip push on to the bar was amazing but, ultimately, doesn't actually count as the ref gave a handball by the striker in the lead up.

It was all Sevilla for the rest of the match as they searched for an equaliser, it was another very nervy game to watch after being in front and looking comfortable. That's a theme of this season I'm not enjoying. In injury time a low cross was punched away by the diving Raya but he misjudged it and the ball looped back towards our goal. Thankfully, it landed on the top of the net and we survived to take the three points.

A great win, a mostly strong performance but a few heart in mouth moments that pushed the heart rate up.

NDV: It's funny how close scoring games make you nervous while you are watching but then the stats suggest a much more comfortable win. We had 14 shots to their 11, 4 on target to their 2. It didn't feel anything like that for the last thirty minutes though. Regardless, we remain top of the group and with the next two games at home we could well seal a place in the knockout stages with a game to spare.

View from The Avenell Club

Saturday 28th October 2023
Sheffield Utd (h) 5-0

It's going to be champagne football all the way today as my mate of 40+ years, Dean, has kindly offered me a ticket in the Avenell Club. Michael and I had the tickets a couple of years ago but I had to drive up so couldn't take full advantage of the excellent bar options. We beat Southampton 3-0 that day and today's opponents don't look like they are going to offer much more of a challenge.

It's an early train ready for the 12:30 stadium opening, then we enjoy numerous glasses of bubbly and some excellent food as we approach the 3pm kick off. A couple of old school mates are also there so it's a bit of a party feeling, but the team selection is a bit of a shock. Kiwior in at the back perhaps the biggest surprise but he actually has a good game, showing some excellent passing and technical ability. To be fair I think even I could've played alongside the imperious Saliba. His reading of the game and physicality are just immense. And I could definitely have played in goal as Sheffield offered nothing going forward. But they are well organised at the back and we struggle to make chances until finally Declan Rice feeds a ball in to Eddie, his first touch is dare I say "Bergkampesque" and he slots home for a very welcome half time lead.

I'd gone for 5-0 on the Skybet Super 6 but all day have been hedging my bets by saying I could also see a nervy 1-0 if we didn't get an early goal. As we get back on the champers discussion turns to whether the flood gates will now open. They do.

Eddie grabs a second after the keeper fluffs a corner, then rifles his hat trick goal in to the top corner from 25 yards. A Viera penalty after an incredibly long VAR check makes it four. The ref didn't originally give the pen and seemed determined not to with the amount of time he took viewing the replays. At least in our posh seats we were getting the replays and pictures the tv audience gets. The rest of the stadium just have to sit there wondering what the bloody hell they are doing. Why can't they show everyone the replays - do they think we'd riot if we saw something we didn't like?!?

Tomiyasu gets his first goal for the club in injury time, I have my predicted 5-0 (forget the 1-0 bit) and we polish off some more wine before making the calamitous decision to go to the pub. A cloudy memory of the journey home but I do recall bumping in to Adrian Dunbar (Line of Duty star) in the pub. What a fantastically generous and accommodating chap he is, happily chatting to us, posing for multiple selfies and even (and I can't believe I asked him to) FaceTiming Mary and saying "Jesus, Mary, Joseph and the wee donkey" to her. Made her day and probably kept me one step away from the dog house! What a great day. Through the magic of text messaging I learn Michael is equally pissed as he turned the whole day in to a festival of beer with his mates and eventually got home late Sunday! Oh to be young again.

NDV: Surprised at the lack of a hangover - obviously good quality champagne. Sheffield Utd really were poor, no shots after the first 20 mins, only 2 all day and none on target. But you can only beat what's in front of you. We move on to West Ham in the EFL Cup in the week.

Not good enough

Wednesday 1st November 2023
EFL Cup West Ham (a) 3-1

A really poor performance, especially from players getting a rare start but who did little to change that. Ramsdale was fouled on the first, made a good save, then no chance on the second and a deflected shot for the third. Trossard and Havertz just never got in to the game, Eddie missed two reasonable chances which would have kept us in the game. Good finish from Ødegaard for our goal but too little too late. We need to put this one behind us, as this was our lowest priority competition, but that doesn't excuse the performance. More creativity and better finishing are required urgently!

NDV: Not much to add, Declan Rice got a load of stick from West Ham fans, I can't say I blame them but he's already showing he's a top class player. Rival fans don't boo good players.

Fuming!

Saturday 4th November 2023
Newcastle (a) 1-0

Michael headed to a pub in London to watch this one, after another gym session. No idea where he gets the energy from. I settled down in front of the tv with a beer hoping to see an improvement over the midweek EFL game.

Newcastle are very strong at home but we absolutely killed their game with solid defending and great possession. They went an hour without a shot. Yes we failed to create enough and 0-0 would've been a fair result but obviously football isn't fair. But this goes beyond bad luck, it was sheer incompetence from the officials. Was the ball out of play, probably not and so we have to accept that one, whilst wondering why their goal line camera isn't positioned to show more of the goal line than just the bit between the sticks. Was there a handball, clearly yes. Was there a push, yes but only with two hands! Was he offside, probably but they apparently couldn't find a camera angle. Ok I'm clutching at straws, but as the ball was obscured by Joelinton, draw a line from him and if the scorer is ahead then it's offside. If he's not ahead then let it go. They spend ages trying to find ways to disallow our goals so why not take a little longer here. I'm fuming because this is the latest in a catalogue of errors we have had this season alone, without even thinking about some of the previous seasons' decisions. Something has to change.

NDV: Still got the hump about it and social media shows it's not just me. Quite a few pundits also saying it was a push, why didn't VAR at least let the on field ref have another look before finalising the decision?

I was a big advocate of introducing VAR, there had been too many high profile errors that changed results so I felt using the technology was a must. The problem is we now have too many high profile errors changing results despite the technology. It ultimately comes down to the people using it and the processes they are employing. VAR is clearly here to stay but the officials have got to get better. Compare how VAR was used in the last World Cup. You hardly noticed it. Why is its use in the Premier League so much more questionable?

It wasn't supposed to be this easy!

Wednesday 8th November 2023
UCL Sevilla (h) 2-0

After all the years of waiting, since Man Utd beat us in the semi final in 2009, I finally get to see another UCL match in the flesh. That said, I don't feel that excited for some reason. Perhaps the crap drive up in heavy London rush hour traffic, perhaps the November chill and dampness in the air, perhaps the number of first team players out with injury. Still there's a light show to look forward to!??

I meet Michael in our seats. He had an equally frustrating journey on the underground, passing through but not stopping at Highbury & Islington and having to walk back from Finsbury Park. I'm armed with my now traditional £5 Pepsi, he's got a couple of pints in after meeting Charlie.

The crowd give a subdued rendition of The Angel, played earlier than usual due to UEFA regulations, but a slightly louder "the Champions!" Rings out at the end of the anthem. Still a few empty seats and the atmosphere is not quite as good as recent games but Arsenal settle in well and dominate. Martinelli has the right back in his pocket and runs past him again and again. Havertz misses a close range header from a corner but Sevilla are poor and offer nothing going forward. Then a sublime, defence splitting pass from Jorginho finds Saka who squares it to Trossard for a classic Arsenal goal. 1-0 at the break.

The second half is much the same, Arsenal in total control but I fear we have seen this before and not come away with a win. What was I thinking? We score an excellent second after Martinelli finds Saka with a great through ball. Saka runs from almost the half way line, cuts back inside the defender, who has clearly never seen him play, and fires into the corner. Now we can relax. Perhaps a few more subs would have been prudent, what with all the injuries, but we see the game out. Sevilla's one and only shot coming in the 97th minute!

NDV: It really was a walk in the park, the group is in our hands along with top spot. Man Utd's late capitulation in Copenhagen is as funny as it is ironic since my last UCL game at the Emirates saw them stroll on to the final at our expense. How far they have fallen. Pep, whose Barcelona team beat them in that final in Rome, is probably the obstacle we will need to overcome if we are to win this competition but I'm getting way ahead of myself now.

We will remember them

Saturday 11th November 2023
Burnley (h) 3-1

Armistice Day demonstrations and the Lord Mayor's Show in Central London mean the trains are messed up, and the roads clogged up, but driving is the best option. So, I'm not on the beer today despite the 3pm kick off. Michael heads to the gym early with Charlie and we agree to meet at the ground. As I'm walking through the turnstile there is an almighty roar as Wolves score an injury time winner against Spurs. The concourse is rocking and everyone is singing in full voice about how Spurs appear to get battered wherever they travel to. Ha ha brilliant start to the day!

We take our seats early as we want to see the Remembrance ceremony. The stadium is only half full when they play The Angel, a bit earlier than usual, so it's a very flat rendition today.

The ceremony is very well organised and the lady who is Arsenal's Operations Manager (I think that's what they said) recites the "we will remember them" poem. She's clearly nervous and misses a bit out but, as someone who served over 20 years in the RAF, I think she's more than earned a pass on that.

Burnley, under Vincent Kompany, don't usually sit deep and they start off pressing us high. However, it soon becomes clear that isn't going to work and they drop off noticeably, but still look like they could have something to offer going forward. As the game settles and Michael and I discuss the finer points he asks me who I think is better, Raya or Ramsdale. Raya makes a good save and distributes the ball out wide with a side swipe kick from his hands. It curls in to the path of Martinelli but is just a little too heavy. "Raya" I answer with a smile. I actually think they are both very good and that there's very little between them, but Raya seems to fit the mould Arteta is after.

A decent first half is drawing to a close, Michael heads off for some refreshment but I decline as I don't want to miss any of the game, a sound decision as Trossard bravely heads us in front before clattering into the post. The crowd are unsure if it's a goal, so is the stadium announcer but eventually he runs the videos on the big screen and declares the goal scorer.

As ever I feel we need a second to make it more comfortable but Burnley grab a deflected equaliser. Shit! This is going to be one of those days. Except, no it's not. Saliba scores a lovely header from a corner three minutes after their equaliser and normal service is restored. The atmosphere is a little more subdued but in block 101 there's singing throughout every game so it's more difficult to judge the overall feeling around the ground. It obviously goes up several notches when there is jeopardy involved, like a late winner or if there is a nasty tackle, but it certainly doesn't feel quiet or like the fabled library. A little kid leads us in the "what do you think of Tottenham" song. We all join in while laughing. "What a lovely kid" I declare, "why can't you be like that Michael?" brings a snigger from the lady next to me.

Zinchenko raises the decibel level with a superb scissor kick goal to put some gloss on the score line, Vieira gets a stupid red card that probably means he won't play again before Christmas, allowing for the three game ban, international break and expected ire of Arteta for jeopardising this game. No panic though as we defend well with ten men and even end the game with nine men while waiting for the thirty seconds required to get an injured player back on. What a ridiculous rule that is. Some poetic justice when the final whistle goes and the ball immediately hits the ref (Michael Oliver) on the head. Three points and we go joint top with City prior to their game at Chelsea tomorrow.

NDV: This will not be a game that lives long in the memory but that's not to say it wasn't enjoyable. We rounded the night off with pizza, beer and a movie and City played the most ridiculous game at Chelsea, ending 4-4, so we are only a point behind them as we break for the internationals.

A very Happy Birthday!

Saturday 25th November 2023
Brentford (a) 0-1

This was always going to be a tricky away fixture and on the eve of my birthday it had the potential to screw up my whole weekend, but thankfully the Arsenal did the business.

Ramsdale, back in goal due to Raya being with us on loan and unable to play against his parent club, was clearly nervous. He had Rice to thank for clearing off the line after giving the ball away. Another error with a throw out left me feeling his time is pretty much up now, sad but something of a fact of life at this level.

We controlled the game, had a Trossard goal rightly disallowed for offside and made several good chances which just wouldn't go in. I'd pretty much settled for a point when Saka crossed late on and there was Havertz at the far post to nod it in. The away fans went crazy as did I, sitting alone in my living room!

BirthdayV: To be honest the game is a bit of a haze, too many pints out of the Perfect Draft the cause of that. But it had always felt like we had control and wouldn't lose. It was just a case of could we break them down and get a winner. We did, and now sit top of the table as a result. Happy Birthday David!

Europe take note

Wednesday 29th November 2023
UCL Lens (h) 6-0

After a few issues during the day, I set off later than planned but luckily the A13 is behaving itself. I get parked up with just enough time to walk to the ground, negotiate the queue and dash up to my seat (via a quick pit stop - I'm of that age) in time to catch the lacklustre rendition of The Angel. It really doesn't work when half the ground is empty but UEFA's rules prevent it being played at the usual time. Michael joins me as The Champions League anthem rings out and we settle in for the match. We need to win to ensure we win the group and, hopefully, avoid a tough draw in the next round.

Within 28 minutes we are 4-0 up, running amok and have sewn it up. I won't run through all the goals but suffice to say the football was sublime. Passing and movement reminiscent of 20 years ago, Ødegaard back to something like his best pulling the strings. And it's our captain who rounds off a brilliant first half with a perfect volley, ending another superb move, to make it 5-0 at the break.

My only concern is that often games that are decided by half time drift aimlessly to a dull conclusion and all the goals so far have been at the other end. I'm greedy, I want some in front of the North Bank!

We control the second half and it seems to make the evening feel warmer than the thermometer suggests. Michael and I chat throughout, there's no jeopardy so we are relaxed and almost taking our eye off the game a little. I feel like the rest of the ground is doing the same, apart from when a couple of idiot Lens fans start throwing flares at club level.

A late penalty is converted by Jorginho, without the trademark hoppy skippy bit, and I have my North Bank goal. I can go home happy now.

NDV: It was a comfortable win but Lens did offer a bit of a threat going forward. In the league we don't get as much time and space, European teams don't seem to have worked that out yet. It's very early days but I feel we could have a good run in this competition, just need to avoid some of the big teams and who knows?

Missed opportunities didn't cost us

Saturday 2nd December 2023
Wolves (h) 2-1

A rare Saturday 3pm kick off but a marathon journey to and from the stadium. I drop Mary at Nicola's on the way up, they're having a day together and a night out, which means I have to drive down Tottenham High Road. Never an enjoyable experience. Then Michael has to pick some stuff up from his office on the way home so a lengthy detour around the West End.

Between the two journeys we did get to see a pretty decent game of football. After arriving a little too close to kick off for comfort, we take our seats in a very chilly North Bank. It's definitely a day for the big coats. Thankfully it isn't long before we are celebrating a goal to help warm us up. Saka works the ball well on the edge of the box, plays a one two with Jesus, then another with Tomi and finishes a persistent move with a right foot strike in to the corner. As the stadium rises and the cheers ring out, a weird glove thumping noise accompanies the goal celebrations.

Then we grab a second and there's not even fifteen minutes on the clock. Another slick passing move in and around the area ends with Zinchenko slipping the ball to Ødegaard who is unmarked on the penalty spot. He slots the ball in to the corner perfectly.

Further chances go begging in both the first and second half, it just feels like wave after wave of Arsenal attacks. I start to get a feeling that a third isn't coming and there is a creeping concern being voiced around me that a Wolves goal could cause a problem. I definitely share that view and the singing on the North Bank is slowly dwindling away, me included, as nerves begin to set in.

Then, inevitably it seems, we shoot ourselves in the foot. Zinchenko dwells too long on the ball, is robbed by a Wolves player and it's in the back of the net. The immediate crowd reaction is one of frustration and annoyance, primarily aimed at Zinchenko. "Why doesn't he just clear it?" I ask Michael. "Just boot it clear". He doesn't respond, his face says it all.

Here we go, another nervy finish that was totally avoidable. But wait, Ødegaard slides the ball through to Eddie and he's away. He side foots the ball past the keeper and we all throw our arms in the air as it heads to the bottom corner. But it strikes the post and rolls clear. Sixty thousand people groan! That was the chance to put the game beyond Wolves, though as it turns out it doesn't matter as we see out injury time and win 2-1.

On the long drive home we discuss our performance today. We conclude we should have been out of sight but the finishing still isn't at the level we need. Some of that is players not quite in the groove yet, but I can't escape the feeling we need an elite striker to finish the moves. How many goals would Wrighty or Henry score in this team.

As Mary is staying the night at Nicola's, I settle down in front of the tv with a take away, a few beers and a movie before reliving the day watching Match of the Day.

NDV: It was a great match, I really enjoyed our football, but the finishing has to improve. We got away with it yesterday but there will be close games where profligacy in front of goal will cost points. Still a long way to go but, as the transfer window is less than a month from opening, there will be inevitable speculation about who we may be able to bring in to take us up a level.

Declan Rice you beauty!

Tuesday 5th December 2023
Luton Town (a) 3-4

I watched this on tv on Amazon, via the Sky box. Michael watched in his room on Apple TV. This is important as it meant I was about 20 seconds behind him, which I didn't realise until very late.

Quick thinking from Jesus and Saka created a chance which Martinelli gladly took and I thought we would run away with it. But Luton hadn't read the script and equalised from a corner, poor marking on our part. Jesus scored from a lovely Ben White cross and we were back to the script.

Second half, another Luton corner, Raya flaps, 2-2. Then Barkley shoots and Raya makes a mess with his hands when his feet would have been a better option. Shit. 3-2. Then Havertz latches on to a delicate Jesus pass and prods it home for 3-3. I'm reluctantly settling for the point now and mute the tv as I don't want to hear the bollocks from the commentator at the final whistle. Time is up but we get a free kick. I hear a muffled "Yes! Get in there" from upstairs. What??? I realise I'm a bit behind on the tv, we couldn't could we? Oh yes we could (well it is panto season) and Declan Rice nods it home for 3-4. I'm left delighted but with that same sense you get when you see a goal go in but are convinced it's offside and that VAR will disallow it only to find it stands. Still a win is a win.

NDV: Amazing game which we were in charge of but let in three goals, which is a bit of a contradiction. I'm not sure I can stand too many games like that!

Missed opportunities cost us this time

Saturday 9th December 2023
Aston Villa (a) 1-0

Watched on tv while tucking in to a new keg on my beer machine, Michael went out to the pub to watch it. Villa took the lead early, I'm not sure switching them around so they attacked the Holt End first half was such a great idea. Chance after chance missed after that, and for most of the game it just felt that the equaliser was inevitable. Unfortunately, it just never came. Focus now turns to a dead rubber in the champions league at PSV.

NDV: Similar to the Newcastle game, all the stats showed we dominated and should have won. The most important stat, the score, says different.

Changes made, same quality shines through

Tuesday 12th December 2023
UCL PSV (a) 1-1

As this was the epitome of a "dead rubber" I expected a number of changes in the starting line-up. Arteta agreed and made eight from the team that started against Villa. PSV have been flying in the Eredivisie, they have won every game so far. That puts the 4-0 thumping we gave them at the Emirates in to some perspective and has, apparently, served to inspire them ever since. Glad we could help chaps!

I've been to PSV for a league game, it's a decent stadium and they generate a good atmosphere. So putting their desire for revenge, the loud crowd, their current excellent form and a much changed Arsenal together and you have the recipe for a definite home win. But this Arsenal were having none of that.

For the first half hour PSV were on top, creating chances and putting us under pressure. A speculative shot from Elneny would have been a collector's item had it not gone just the wrong side of the post. Then, just before half time, Nelson played a good one two and charged towards the box. He found Eddie in a little bit of space, that was all he needed to take control and fire the ball in to the corner of the net for his first UCL goal. I feel like I've been a bit harsh on Eddie at times. He's a decent player, capable of scoring in tight situations, but I just feel the squad has developed beyond him. I'm sure he'll have a long career in the Premier League, that alone shows he is an elite footballer, but I don't see that being at Arsenal beyond this season.

PSV came out strong in the second half and equalised within five minutes. After that they had the better of the game, putting us under pressure. We had a goal disallowed for offside from a free kick, they had a late chance to win it but fired wide. Then we could have, and probably should have, won it right at the end but Trossard had his shot saved and Kiwior blasted the rebound over.

So, honours even. A decent result everything considered. We won the group and progress to the knock out round in the new year.

NDV: We actually had the lion's share of possession but their 17 shots to our 12 shows the pressure we were under. We're not used to conceding that many shots this season but with the changes it was always likely we would not be at our absolute best, especially with Rice missing from the start. Interesting choice to bring him on at centre half, perhaps a sign he could be asked to play there at some stage in the league. I'm confident we can go deep in this competition, that's more than Newcastle and Man Utd will do! For now we can put it to bed and concentrate on all things domestic, after we find out who we have in the next round.

Football and Family

Sunday 17th December 2023
Brighton (h) 2-0

A busy week in which me and three old work mates drove to Genk for a Europa Conference League match, and piss up obviously. I head off to the match with Mary, who I'm dropping at a family party which Michael and I will be joining later.

Surprisingly light traffic allows me enough time to finally meet the newest addition to our family, Emile. The one year old first born of my (Spurs supporting!!!) nephew Adam and partner Lara surely should have the middle names Smith and Rowe.

I walk through the turnstiles at the Emirates and am about to text Michael to see where he is. Suddenly the big lump jumps on me, frightening the life out of me, having apparently been queuing next to me with neither of us noticing.

We grab a soft drink so we can go straight to our seats, Michael reflects that more people must be passing tickets on as the ground is pretty much full as the Angel is belted out. The club's policy around ticket utilisation seems to be working.

Arsenal start well, pushing forward and pressing Brighton, who to be fair play confidently around their own area. We create chance after chance but lack finishing prowess and effective decision making. Brighton barely get a sniff going forward as Saliba and big Gabriel give young Evan Ferguson a life lesson. There's a growing sense of frustration in the crowd, quite a bit of singing but not everyone joining in as the tension mounts, we've been here before - missed chances then a sucker punch. When Arteta gets booked the frustration turns to anger and the volume increases noticeably as we all sing the Arteta song. I stop to listen and it feels like the whole of the North Bank are joining in, making the hairs on the back of my neck stand up a little.

Michael disappears for a half time pint and I chat to the young fella next to me (not a season ticket seat, new person every game). We agree there's goals in this for us but that Brighton, who have scored in every game this season, are likely to be better second half.

10 minutes in to the second half and half of our prediction is proved correct as Jesus heads in at the back post, unmarked from a corner. The relief is palpable, a real outpouring of emotion all around us. Now we need another one!

Brighton have plenty of the ball but we are solid defensively in the main. One chance at the near post is flicked past Raya and hits the side netting but for a second the Brighton fans (and me) think it's in. Phew!

Subs made, Eddie and Trossard on. The latter retains the ball well deep in our half, finds Ødegaard who in turn finds Eddie in space. He lays it through to Kai who calmly slots it in the corner past the on rushing keeper. 2-0 and the Kai Havertz song quickly gathers pace. Again, I stop singing to listen and it's loud! There's a definite air of joy now though, you can sense the smiles in the words.

More subs to break play up, more Arsenal chances, notably a decent effort from Emile (not the one year old one obviously).

Final whistle, top of the league for at least an hour until Liverpool slaughter United. As we applaud the players off Michael asks for my player of the match. I'm torn between Ødegaard and Rice. Michael espouses the theory Rice is now worth more like £200m and that we should give West Ham another £20m so as not to appear to have taken the piss. It's hard to argue with his logic.

We head back to my brother's house to see the little fella again and begrudgingly take the piss out of the Spurs fan Adam. Well not that begrudgingly, though as ever he takes it in good spirit despite his uncle trying to teach Emile to sing "fucking hate Tottenham". Emile does seem to like the Arsenal badge though, there's hope for the lad yet!

NDV: the stats show how dominant, and wasteful, we were in front of goal. Arteta commented how we need to be better with the chances we make so I'm sure he'll be working with the team on that. United did the unthinkable and got a 0-0 at Anfield so we stay top. Next game - Liverpool at Anfield. I'd take a draw but with this defence who knows what is possible?

We are definitely title contenders!

Saturday 23rd December 2023
Liverpool (a) 1-1

We have had a family tradition for the last few years where the four of us (Mary, Nicola, Michael and me) have a meal out on the last Saturday before Christmas. Some clever planning meant we left time free in case this match was switched to a 5:30pm kick off - which it duly was. But with an 8pm dinner reservation at Rules (the oldest restaurant in London) we had to find a pub in town to watch the game. The Horatia on Holloway Road was the obvious answer as it's a short direct tube ride to Covent Garden.

So we settled in at a table, a festive Guinness in hand and got the perfect start when big Gabi nodded in a free kick for 1-0. Then the expected onslaught came from the home team, but actually it was quite different to last season. Yes they had chances, yes we rode our luck a bit (Ødegaard handling should definitely have been a penalty) but we were always a threat going forward. Last season we hung on and escaped with a point. This time we went toe to toe with Liverpool, probably the strongest team at home in the Premier League. A draw was, in my opinion, a fair result. The only thing to leave a bitter taste in my mouth was the pork scratchings Michael insisted on eating with his beer. Yuk!

So a decent result, a quick dash to Rules and Christmas starts in earnest. Top of the league, even Klopp described us as "so strong". This is a real title challenge, top for Christmas. Excellent.

NDV: The memory of the game is a bit of a blur, not helped by the cocktails and wine that flowed afterwards. It's always more nervy when watching live on tv but I did feel confident and the stats bear out how well we contained a very strong rival.

How did we not score?!

Thursday 28th December 2023
West Ham (h) 0-2

After a lovely Christmas we had planned to go up by train and have a couple of festive beers but you just cannot trust TFL, especially at this time of year. So a day off the booze and a quick drive up, dropping Nicola home after she had spent Christmas with us.

The atmosphere was jovial and expectant, I was really certain we would win comfortably but a balls up at the back and another VAR debate about whether the ball was out ends with an early goal for the Hammers. From my seat it was definitely out, later pictures shared by the bloke in front with the best mobile reception going also seemed to confirm it.

But there's no point wasting time blaming the inept referee (again!). We simply failed to take our chances. Saka, Jesus, Trossard all missed good opportunities. West Ham doubled the lead from a corner - "I've got a bad feeling about this" I had proclaimed to Michael seconds before the ball was headed in. Michael's expletives that followed were partly due to the immediate feeling of annoyance and partly due to the inevitable grief he could now expect from his Hammers supporting mate.

Not the result we expected, or wanted, but fair play to Moyes for getting his tactics spot on. Hopefully this was a blip.

At least the drive home was quick and the late turkey sandwich ended the day on a high note.

NDV: 30 shots but no goals. The issue is clear, we need the front three and supporting cast to step up to last season levels or we need to dip in to the market in January. We have had a few poor results despite controlling games but sooner, rather than later, we need to start scoring more.

WTF was that performance?!

Sunday 31st December 2023
Fulham (a) 2-1

I watched this game on tv in a bit of a post Christmas funk, you know where you just lounge about all day eating peanuts. We didn't have any real plans for New Years' Eve so this just felt like a way to while away the hours waiting for midnight.

Fulham aren't in great form so here was an opportunity to finish the year on top of the league, an opportunity we passed on. More worryingly the performance was abject, despite a scrappy early Saka goal to give us a lead. After that we just seemed to forget how to play.

Eddie up front was anonymous, Saka and Martinelli struggled and even Declan Rice and Ødegaard were below par. We had 30 minutes left when Fulham went ahead, we never looked like scoring. How can a team that swatted Brighton aside and were so good at Anfield produce such a below par performance just days later? Fatigue? I don't buy that as we actually had quite big gaps between matches, although this was only three days after the West Ham game. But very little travelling required and several players rotated, plus a desire to respond to the West Ham defeat, here was a great chance for three precious points.

Arteta surprised me in that he didn't throw Smith Rowe on. He surely has to be sold if he isn't trusted in games like this when we need something different. Or is he still struggling with injury?

We started throwing crosses in late on, a bit pointless after Havertz had gone off and without a presence in the box most of the time. If we can afford a striker we need to get one. If we can't we need to look for other options. Swap the wide men over now and again, push Havertz up front for the last 10 minutes, play ESR as he will look to take players on - something we just aren't doing this season. Whatever the answer, Arteta needs to figure it out quickly or the league will be out of reach. Liverpool and City are both in good form.

NDV: We have taken one point off Fulham in the two league games despite leading in both. Not the sign of potential champions but we are still in the mix and there is half a season left. FA Cup next. Happy New Year!

"We need a killer"

Sunday 7th January 2024
FAC Liverpool (h) 0-2

Thanks to another planned strike on TFL the advice was to complete journeys by 5:30pm. Bit difficult when the second half was due to kick off at that time! So we are back in the car for this one.

The temperature has dropped significantly after a very mild Christmas and New Year so actually the idea of travelling by car is not such a bad one.

Michael and I arrive at the ground a good 40 minutes or so before kickoff, so we can at least have a relaxed drink before making our way to our seats. The team news is a little surprising in that Havertz is playing upfront as a traditional number nine (ish) and Nelson replaces Martinelli on the left wing. Kiwior is at left back and Rambo is finally back in goal.

We make our way to our seats and I notice there are a lot of people already in theirs, a little bit unusual as it's still a good 15 minutes before kickoff. For some unknown reason Michael decides to walk into row 24 rather than row 25 where our seats are, then proceeds to have a debate with the man he believes is sitting in his seat when actually it's Michael that is in the wrong place. The confusion is quickly resolved, and we sit in our normal seats. There are a lot of unfamiliar faces around me and there's something different about the atmosphere that I can't put my finger on. Maybe a heightened sense of anticipation, people seem more excited than normal. Possibly more "first timers". I think this may be due to the mix up and problems they had with the Cup Ticket scheme, something that we had issues with ourselves. When they play The Angel, the first couple of lines are sung with gusto but after that many of the people around me clearly don't know the words. Nevertheless, the game gets underway and Arsenal are 100% at it right from the start. A fantastic pass from Ramsdale straight down the middle to Nelson puts him in one on one with the keeper. The ball is bouncing and my immediate feeling is that he should try and lob the keeper who is some way off of his line. Instead he dribbles round the keeper, but miscontrols and ends up trying to score from the touchline (impossible angle) when he should've pulled the ball back for one of the two forwards bursting into the area. Still it's a good sign that we are likely to create chances which we in fact we do for the next 10 or 15 minutes. Unfortunately the recent profligacy in front of goal continues. Liverpool have their chances and always seem to carry a threat when going forward. Trent hits the bar on one of these occasions, but the first half is pretty much one way traffic in our favour.

At half-time the stats show we are very much on top, but once again, it's the most important stat we are lacking in. 0–0 against this Liverpool team is not a comfortable feeling. As expected Liverpool are much better in the second half and the game more even, but still Arsenal continue to create good chances which they consistently fail to take. After the last couple of games you just know what's coming. Sure enough, with about 10 minutes left Liverpool get a free kick on the left, the delivery is good and the ball ends up in the back of our net courtesy, as it turns out, of the unfortunate Kiwior. Arteta brings on Eddie, but he has a very poor record of scoring as a substitute. As it turns out he only touches the ball once in the remainder of the game. More subs at 87 minutes looks like a bit of a desperate attempt to get a draw, which neither side really wants, and I can't help thinking that it is a lot to ask of the players coming on, namely Smith–Rowe and Trossard. We push hard for an equaliser but right at the end of injury time Liverpool break and finish the game off with a well taken goal.

All in all a very disappointing day and we are out of another competition which I was hoping we would have a good run in, if not actually win it. Both Michael and I keep our own counsel on the way home showing we are more than a little frustrated with both today and recent results. There is a tweet from Ian Wright, that simply says "we need a killer". If anyone knows about scoring goals it's Wrighty and I think he is 100% correct. The problem is where do you get a top-class striker in January when you have FFP to worry about. The indication from Arteta in his press conference is that we will need to make do with the players we have rather than expect a shiny new signing in the January window.

We have a two week break now until the next league game and the team are off to Dubai for some warm weather training and rest. Let's just hope Arteta can pick them up and reignite them for the next run of games, because we need to get back on the winning track very quickly or this league campaign is going south.

NDV: whilst I'm disappointed to have been knocked out of the cup, it does mean that even after the two week break, our fixture list will be relatively light and hopefully that means we can get one or two players fit and performing. I'm steering clear of social media, because there is a lot of crap being posted, including calls to sack the manager. People need to remember how bad we were when Arteta joined and how far we have come under his tenure before giving up on him so easily. Hopefully we can come back firing on all cylinders and spank Palace in two weeks.

We're back!

Saturday 20th January 2024
Crystal Palace (h) 5-0

An early kick off means parking is more difficult and with the trains behaving themselves for once it's an easy decision to use TFL and have a couple of beers. Except the plans are impacted when Michael fails a late fitness test having been struggling with flu for a couple of days. Unfortunately the decision comes too late for me to pass his ticket on as the exchange closes 3 hours before kickoff, so I'm flying solo on this one.

Ironically, all the moves the club has made to stop touts and encourage full attendance mean, on this occasion, there's an empty seat next to me that I could have filled easily. There are also still numerous touts outside the Arsenal station offering tickets for sale, so more work clearly needed.

I arrive in good time and decide to take the opportunity to wander round the upper concourse, primarily looking for a proper sausage (not hot dog) for my late breakfast. Not realising there is a suitable concession counter 10 yards anti clockwise from section 101 and proceeding to walk clockwise round the entire ground. At the Clock End I see the club shop window selling scarves and the like. The Ashburton Army have put out a plea for everyone to bring a scarf to hold up at the start to boost the atmosphere, and it's very noticeable that most people have complied. I decide to treat myself to a £20 scarf (knock off for a fiver outside!) and am rewarded for my loyalty when the young woman selling it to me asks if I am a member so she can reduce the price to £13.50. Bargain.

A cheeky beer to wash down breakfast and I take my seat, actually Michael's as I'm chatting to the young fella who sits next to us. Friendly chap, gives me a good steer on overcoming the ticket exchange issue. I really must ask him his name, it's been 3 seasons now after all.

We are fielding a strong team, Jesus and Zinchenko are back but Trossard is in for (we find out later an injured) Martinelli. The scarf thing is a bit flat around us though has pretty good traction around the rest of the ground, especially in the lower tier.

A fast start suggests the week in the Dubai sunshine has been worthwhile and after just 10 mins a perfect corner from Rice is powered home by Gabriel. That's followed by another couple of chances from set pieces before we grab a second from Saka's great corner, Gabriel heading in off the keeper. It actually feels like this one is in the bag as Palace are woeful and we are in control. But with recent history I'm not counting the chickens just yet.

In the second half Palace seem slightly rejuvenated and apply some pressure, but this proves their undoing as a corner is comfortably caught by Raya before his excellent throw sets Jesus away. It's two on two with Trossard busting a gut to get in to the box, Jesus finds him perfectly. Trossard skips inside the defender, who slips out of the game, and fires high beyond the keeper. Top quality break away football, we all roar with delight and now I am sure the points are safe. Except, hold on. VA poxy R. Checking for Trossard offside. When I watch the replay later it's absolutely clear in real time he's onside just using the grass lines as a guide. Why it took them so long to confirm is unbelievable. Perhaps they were looking for some other reason, anything, just to disallow it. The more times the decisions are wrong, or take an inordinate amount of time to be made, the more it plays to the conspiracy theories. Personally, I think they are just poor at their jobs. Yes it's pressure, yes you are in the public spotlight, yes you want to take time to get it correct but the growing trend of poor decisions just makes me think they need to refresh the people. Just have one qualified, experienced ref to arbitrate on the rules and then have tech savvy people (mixed age, race and gender) with fast track rules training to speed up the whole thing. Ideally, an ex player who can tell the difference when someone accidentally injures someone as opposed to deliberately going for them. Rant over. It won't be the last time.

Back to the football, and Arteta makes all 5 subs, including ESR who gets a massive cheer and looks very sharp. Martinelli is put through on the keeper by Eddie and does his best Thierry Henry impression to make it 4-0. Then Jorginho puts him in again and he repeats the finish for 5-0. Just what the doctor ordered.

I decide to have a celebratory pint and watch the highlights on the lower concourse rather than queue up to get in to the station. Then it's a leisurely journey home listening to the mad American Elliot on the Arsenal Vision Podcast Instant Reaction. Pretty good day all round.

NDV: Match of the Day didn't show a great deal of the game, strange considering there were only two games today. They spent more time analysing Ødegaard adjusting his socks at corners, offering the suggestion this was a sign to the team to tell them which routine we were using. Weird.

Deja vu!

Tuesday 30th January 2024
Nottingham Forest (a) 1-2

This had all the makings of a banana skin, or "trap" game to our American friends - Elliot @ Arsenal Vision will be proud of me. However, this season we seem to be winning the games we normally lose, and vice versa.

Surprisingly, ESR is in the starting lineup and has a decent game. The first half pattern was set early, it's attack v defence with Arsenal in complete control but, at times, it was a bit slow paced. This is a criticism that has been levelled regularly this season, especially Zinchenko who seemed to always take several touches instead of the one/two we see when Arsenal are at their fluent best. Forest were content to literally sit in their own penalty area while we horse shoed around them. Clearly their plan was to hit us on the break which they only managed once resulting in a wild shot over the bar. Then for the last 5 minutes or so of the first half we increased the pace and tempo, creating a couple of chances. I didn't want the half to end.

0-0 at the break but in control and with the crowd quietened. Then the breakthrough from a clever quick throw by Zinchenko and Jesus squeezed the ball in past Turner from a very tight angle. Definitely a keeper error but we'll take that all day long. And it capped a decent performance from Jesus who had earlier hit the post at the end of a fantastic move, then blasted another effort over after some sublime skill flicking over two defenders. A second goal from a brilliant breakaway when Jesus found Saka who shot across the keeper and it felt like the game was won. Just like the game at the Emirates I relaxed and started thinking that perhaps a third or even fourth goal to boost the goal difference was possible. Then with five minutes to go we sloppily concede a goal and it's "squeaky bum" time. Why do you always seem to do this to us Arsenal?

Arteta made changes, Jorginho and Trossard brought some calmness and control. Eddie had little opportunity but I do find his pressing infuriating. Someone needs to show him a video of how Ødegaard does it, sprint don't jog! Apart from one weak shot which Raya collected comfortably, the feared Forest onslaught never materialised so it's a good three points that hopefully builds more confidence ahead of the home game with Liverpool on Sunday.

NDV: A good win but the online narrative is that we still struggle against teams defending deep. Many believe it's this lack of a cutting edge that will prevent us overhauling City and Liverpool who both also won. I do think there are times we need to push Havertz up top if plan A isn't working, but that should be a last 15 minutes ploy. In this game our quick thinking (from the throw) worked against a defence that inevitably was tiring, probably more mentally than physically, so you could argue plan A worked. Focus now is the big game against Liverpool.

Back in the title race!

**Sunday 4th February 2024
Liverpool (h) 3-1**

A massive game that can effectively end our title hopes if we lose, or see us right back in the mix with a win. More TFL/C2C strikes and issues mean we're back in the car again which helps a bit as Mary decides to have a girlie day with Nicola - code for a boozy roast lunch out with cocktails and wine. So I drop Mary off and head to the Emirates to meet Michael who has obviously been at the gym. Traffic is a bit sticky after an accident on the A13 and a bit heavy along Tottenham High Road so I arrive at the ground a bit later than I'd hoped. Michael is in his seat having picked me up a Diet Coke (in a bottle with a top?!?!), and it's noticeable that the ground is pretty full 15 minutes before kick off.

As the teams emerge the noise volume increases and The Angel rings out as loudly as I can remember this season. Well the crowd are definitely up for this, and so are the team as we get off to a fast start, pressing high and moving the ball well. An early break sees Martinelli out run Konate and cross well, Saka is just unable to get his head on it properly and it goes wide. Then a lovely quick passing move finds Ødegaard who sets Havertz away with a perfect pass. I didn't fancy him to beat Allison who is probably the best keeper around one on one, I was right but Allison's block falls to Saka who controls and fires home. The place goes wild, the noise is deafening. Big game, even bigger atmosphere.

We continue to play well for the rest of the first half, highlighted by Ben White performing cheeky turns and nutmegs, but I start to get a feeling that we need to fashion better chances at the end of some great possession and passing moves. As stoppage time is almost up a speculative ball over the top is marshalled well by Saliba but he should clear it instead of waiting for Raya to collect. Diaz pokes the ball, it hits Gabriel and ends up in the net. Bollocks!

I spend half time feeling we have blown a great advantage, people around me argue over culpability - whether Raya or Saliba is most at fault. I hope we can put this behind us but the first 15 minutes of the second half sees Liverpool take the initiative and create a couple of good chances. Klopp makes three early subs but this seems to allow us to get some control back. A long ball forward, something we haven't tried too often, looks easy for Van Dyke to head clear. He lets it bounce and waits for the keeper to clear but a subtle nudge from Martinelli causes mayhem and the ball drops at his feet perfectly for him to slot it in from the edge of the box. Again, the crowd go nuts, the two young blokes next to me are jumping all over each other and me. I can forgive that. As the goal is replayed everyone cheers each time the Liverpool players clatter in to each other. I'm sure it is replayed more times than goals usually are, top shithousery from the stadium staff.

It's going to be a tense ending, Liverpool push forward but we drop in to a good shape and look pretty solid. I say to Michael that there is bound to be a chance or two for us on the break, partly justifying Nelson coming on for the injured Saka. As one such break looks set to materialise Konate pulls Kai back and collects his second yellow card. We wave bye bye to him and it now feels like we have a gilt edged chance to win this one. It's still a bit nervy though, or is that just me? In injury time the ball goes wide to Trossard, he turns two players and leaves them in his wake as he sprints toward goal. There's no one up with him so he just keeps going and hits a strong left footed shot low and somehow the keeper allows it to go through his legs. For the third time the ground erupts, this one is even more passionate. I'm jumping on Michael, deep down you know that has sealed the win, the relief is immense and it pours out of everyone. And for once the ground is still almost full so the noise reverberates around the stadium, cheers accentuated by the slapping of seats folding up as everyone rises to their feet. The feeling of complete joy, the feeling of belonging with thousands of like minded people, that moment of what is probably best described as sheer ecstasy. And that, Gary Neville, Jamie Carragher, Chris Sutton, Richard Keyes and all the other killjoys, is why we love football. And it's why the players and manager, who are under so much more pressure than us mere mortals, should celebrate a tremendous victory in a massively important game. And if you don't like it, we don't care.

The stadium DJ plays the Angel at the end and my voice is croaking as I bellow it out. Get in there! A long drive home through heavy traffic cannot deflate us and the takeaway and a couple of beers in front of Match of the Day 2 is the perfect way to end the day.

NDV: we restricted Liverpool to their lowest xG of the season apparently and, despite having only 47% possession (I was surprised at that), the underlying stats show we were well worth the win. Loads of nonsense about Arsenal over celebrating, especially Ødegaard grabbing the camera off club photographer Stuart and taking his picture in front of the North Bank. The bloke is a lifelong fan, remember his team talk before the NLD in the "All or Nothing" series? What on earth is the problem? And why is what Arsenal do any different or worse than De Zerbi, Pep or even Klopp when he ran on the pitch v Everton? Oh, I see, it's because it's Arsenal. Ridiculous. But for the best comment on this, listen to the Arsecast (do that anyway, it's brilliant) and the reaction from James from Gunnerblog to Chris Sutton. Comedy gold.

Really respectful Rice

Sunday 11th February 2024
West Ham (a) 0-6

After City and Liverpool both won, as expected, this was a pressure game and pretty much a must-win. Well the team didn't disappoint.

More injuries meant that, despite a strong 11, the bench was more than a little light. More on that later.

I thought we started a little nervously, giving the ball away early, but then we started to find some rhythm. Chances started to come our way, Trossard with a header over and a thunderbolt well saved, Saka way off with a header then shooting just wide when one on one with the keeper. Then a great header from a corner by Saliba broke the deadlock. That said we still missed chances and even Alan Smith on tv commentary made the point we could come to regret them.

Trossard set Saka away and he was brought down for a clear penalty. As he stepped up to take it I was very nervous for him, thinking back to his previous penalty miss at this ground. You felt if he could score then our defensive strength should see us get the win, but a miss and the atmosphere and perhaps momentum would change dramatically. Saka made no mistake and after that it felt like West Ham couldn't see a way back. With Gabriel heading a third and Trossard blasting in a fourth it was game over before half time. A fair few West Ham fans obviously agreed as they headed home.

I was half expecting the second half to play out without incident but Arsenal had very different ideas and kept pushing. A brilliant Saka goal, his 51st in the EPL along with 49 assists - marvellous achievements for such a young player. Then Declan Rice capped the day with a long range scorcher. He chose not to celebrate understandably, and fair play to the West Ham fans who stood and applauded him for that.

6-0 (six) and suddenly the goal difference deficit was wiped out.

Arteta brought on all of his allowed subs including a very confident looking Nwaneri who was constantly getting on the ball and interchanging with Ødegaard like he is a veteran. He looks promising but as he's still only 16 will need careful management.

A fantastic result and performance but a long way to go. You have to see City as favourites at this stage but we are in with a chance and the form looks to have taken a decidedly upward trajectory since the short winter break.

It's just a shame the 49ers (my NFL team) couldn't win the Super Bowl later in the day.

NDV: Twitter/X awash with the usual mix of hilarious memes and comments taunting rival fans plus a load of absolute bullshit from far too many dickheads who should probably be better supervised. Biggest away win in my lifetime, though I do recall we scored 6 at Villa in the early 80s. Pretty good day and great to hear the Arsenal fans in good voice and spirits throughout the second half.

Who needs a new striker?

**Saturday 17th February 2024
Burnley (a) 0-5**

The narrative over the last few months has been about how Arsenal desperately need to buy a top quality striker if we are to have any hope of winning anything. The January transfer window came and went and no new signings appeared. But it's starting to look like the stinging criticism, plus a week in the Dubai sunshine, has reinvigorated our front line. Five wins in five, scored 21 goals, goal difference improved by +19 and a defence so solid we have only had 2 shots on target against us in the last three games.

Yes you can argue Burnley are a very poor side and that West Ham are in dreadful form but if this was City putting in these performances and getting these results everyone would be singing their praises.

This match was a 3pm Saturday kick off so I wouldn't have been able to watch it anyway but I had arranged a weekend away in Edinburgh with old work mates (catching up with other work mates who live up there) anyway so this wasn't a problem. In fact I kept up with the score whilst sitting behind the goal at Tynecastle watching Hearts beat Motherwell. Despite being a relatively small ground it was a great atmosphere, helped by the away fans who had a drum and didn't stop banging it. Decent game, full stadium and a great day out, especially in the pubs before and after with Mark, Jimmy and Joe. Massive thank you to Sharon and Andy for queuing for the tickets even though they didn't go to the game. And a quick hello to

Diana who was also part of the gang for the brilliant night we had on the Friday.

As for the 5-0, I watched the goals on Sky, great opener from Ødegaard after 4 minutes set us up well. Saka's slightly unconvincing penalty put us well ahead by half time, then his second put the game to bed. Trossard finally grabbed a goal, after missing a couple he should've done better with, and Havertz put the seal on it with a great individual goal.

It's getting close at the top and we are right in the mix. New striker? To be honest I would like to see someone come in who brings a physical presence and is capable of scoring a hat full, but that will be for the summer. For now I'm enjoying watching a free scoring Arsenal and just hoping we can keep this up.

NDV: I listened to the Arsenal Vision Instant Reaction podcast on the flight home and it certainly sounds like Arsenal were in complete control. The pod is understandably a bit more relaxed after a win but always worth a listen. Let's hope for more of the same after the UCL game away in Porto in the week.

Reality check

Wednesday 21st February 2024
UCL Porto (a) 1-0

I settled down to watch the match on tv, after an early dinner, feeling confident that the long wait for a win in a UCL knockout round may be almost over. Wrong!

Right from the start we didn't look ourselves. A pass to Declan Rice while he was looking the other way, and moaning at Saka for his apparent failure to move in to space on the wing, resulted in him losing the ball and then lunging to try to win it back. Yellow card. Though to be fair I thought Declan still played quite well even with the threat of a sending off hanging over him.

But the scene was set. We were ponderous, cautious and happy to play "horse shoe" football. It reminded me of the games leading up to the winter break. Porto are not having their best season but have a good home record. It seemed as if we had come in to this game thinking we would control it and happily take a draw if that's how it ends up.

But when they managed to spring the trap and break they looked so much more threatening than we did. They missed a sitter and we just continued to waste one set piece after another.

Michael had been caught up at work so watched the first half on his phone on the train home. He joined me for the second half and we both had the feeling that we would either draw or win this one, despite the lack of clear cut chances. It was a pretty dull game to be honest.

Then as we entered injury time I was thinking a 0-0 is ok, though had a sneaking suspicion there was a sting in the tail of this one. So it proved, a series of mistakes led to a goal that was of much higher quality than everything that had gone before. Bollocks!

NDV: No shots on target, lowest percentage time of ball in play in UCL, most fouls conceded. Just some of the stats from a pretty woeful night. Porto used every trick in the book to slow the game and prevent us from playing, including soaking the pitch like Liverpool did at Anfield. But that's all part of the game, we have to learn how to deal with it not moan about it being unfair. Actually, Arteta didn't bemoan the Porto tactics but he was clearly unhappy with our performance. Now we have to wait three weeks for the return leg but at least that gives us time to get some of the injured players back. For now we lick our wounds and look forward to another potentially frustrating opponent in Newcastle who come to the Emirates on Saturday.

Back in the groove

Saturday 24th February 2024
Newcastle (h) 4-1

First off I have to say that I think an 8pm kick off on a Saturday night is a ridiculous time to play a Premier League match. But if you want a raucous atmosphere then giving people the whole day to get out on the lash is ideal.

Personally, I was driving so didn't have a drink beforehand. The thought of travelling home late on Saturday after the game, likely getting in to last train territory or a £70 Uber, was not one I was keen on. Michael went up early to the gym despite feeling a bit rough and we met in our seats, in what was a pretty full stadium, just before the teams emerged. I said to him I reckoned the majority of the crowd were pissed but it did make for a rousing rendition of The Angel and a real tingling of excitement as the game kicked off.

A combination of feeling we owed Newcastle one for what happened at their place, and the need to put the midweek defeat out of everyone's minds, had us starting at 100 mph. We chased and harried the defence and forced early mistakes and turnovers. Havertz and Ødegaard very much leading the line. The breakthrough came from a corner, obviously. Big Gabi headed powerfully, the keeper made a decent save but the defenders were all over the place and managed to knock the ball just over the line. The crowd went mad, "1-0 to the Arsenal" rang out and you could feel the team just had their confidence back. We passed and moved leaving Newcastle chasing shadows and then a delightful Jorginho chip was seized upon by

Martinelli behind the defence. He squared it and Havertz came rushing in to slot home. Queue the Havertz song, again it was very loud.

I'm greedy, I wanted a third but said to Michael it would be good to get one just after the break to undo any changes they may make at half time. As it was, Newcastle had a decent spell of possession and started to push forward in the final few minutes of the first half. A chance for Almiron to run through one on one looked very dangerous but Raya stood tall and Almiron seemed to run out of ideas and the ball was cleared without him actually shooting. I think it was offside anyway.

Newcastle never really threatened that much in the second half and we put the game beyond doubt with a typical Saka goal, twisting and turning the defender before firing home. A bit surprising the keeper and defender on the line didn't do better but who cares. A fourth for Kiwior from a corner and everyone completely relaxed and decided to enjoy the rest of the game with a few piss taking songs. I particularly enjoyed "you can stick your Saudi money up your arse" and "who put the ball in the geordies' net, half the fucking team did". Arteta made changes to rest a few for more important games to come but it felt like the rhythm was broken a little and a late consolation goal was conceded, albeit scored by Joe Willock so I wasn't too bothered.

The drive home was nice and quick and I finished the evening off with a nice cold beer watching Match of the Day and enjoying reliving the game. Maybe Saturday night football isn't as bad as I thought after all.

NDV: Some obscure but interesting stats coming out of the game. First team to score 2 goals in seven consecutive halves of football in Premier League history, Saka the first Arsenal player to score in five consecutive league games in 9 years and the first English player to do so since Wrighty. There was a lot of pressure to get this win, Liverpool and City had both won their games so any points dropped would have been bad news. We've got a light schedule through March ending with the away game at City so we need to use the time to get as many injured players back and performing as possible.

Record breakers

Monday 4th March 2024
Sheffield Utd (a) 0-6

It's Monday Night Football on Sky with Thierry Henry as the guest. This calls for an early dinner so I can be sat down on the sofa in time to watch all the pre match stuff. Michael is still feeling poorly so while he waits for the next doctor's appointment he's in bed coughing and spluttering and missing what turned out to be another superb away day for the Arsenal.

Arteta named an unchanged side and the good news is that Jesus, Partey and Vieira are all back on the bench.

Whilst I'm expecting a win I do think it's going to be a lot more difficult than the social media expectation of a thrashing. I was wrong. Within the first couple of minutes we apply pressure and hit the bar. Within 5 minutes we are ahead through Ødegaard. Within 15 minutes it's 3-0 from an own goal forced by Saka and a deflected shot from Martinelli. By half time it's 5-0, a very well taken goal from Havertz after Martinelli had robbed the defender and set him away. Then Rice slotted home from Saka's pull back and everyone is tweeting Elliot at The Arsenal Vision podcast asking if the famed 10-0 is actually on.

My brother texts me how nice it is of Sky to show Arsenal's training session, it does feel like that. Carragher is full of how poor Sheffield Utd are, hardly a mention of how good we have been. I wonder how he would have described a Liverpool 5-0 first half lead?

As expected Arteta makes changes, Saka off at half time, Vieira on. Ben White makes it 6-0 and then is replaced by Cedric. Partey and Jesus also get some much needed minutes. Partey looks very rusty but it's great he can come in to a game that is already won, rather than have to make his errors in a meaningful part of a game.

The stadium is emptying rapidly, some had actually left after just 15 minutes. The Arsenal fans sing about "stadiums are empty everywhere we go", I love football fan humour!

Sky inform us that we are the first team in English top division history to score 5 or more goals in 3 successive away fixtures. We have also scored 2 or more in 8 consecutive halves, another record. We equalled our record away league win, set against West Ham last month. 7-0 away is our best ever away win, in the Cup Winners' Cup in 1993. But, while breaking records is nice, it's a trophy we want the most.

A great win, I watch the after match analysis and conclude Ødegaard really is a special talent.

NDV: Another brilliant performance and display of clinical finishing. The form since the winter break has been exceptional (Porto aside). Saka was apparently feeling sick and Martinelli got a kick so hopefully both will be ok for the next fixture. We have Brentford next where a win will lift us to top, maybe only for a few hours until City got to Anfield. I'm expecting Brentford to be much better organised at the back and to offer a very different threat going forward. I'm really looking forward to Saturday night at the Emirates, fingers crossed Michael has shrugged off his illness and is sitting next to me.

Kai Havertz scores again!

Saturday 9th March 2024
Brentford (h) 2-1

    Michael passes a late fitness test and we drive up together, though he's still not right and only breaks his silence with the occasional coughing fit. A bad accident on the A13 elongates the journey but that's a very minor inconvenience compared to the poor sod who was in the badly damaged car. Hopefully everyone got out ok.
    We arrive just in time to join a very long queue to enter the ground. It seems much less organised and more of a free for all; you just know we are all thinking the same thing - "I'm going to miss kick off".
    Luckily we get in and are climbing the stairs to row 25 as the teams emerge. Michael and I join in with the singing of the Angel but he's wheezing from his chest problems and I'm wheezing because I just climbed all those stairs!
    Brentford are expected to be more organised and offer more threat than recent opponents but Arsenal get off to the now customary fast start, forcing a couple of corners. Brentford are sitting deep but when they get the ball they go long to the two strikers who are giving Gabriel and Saliba a real physical battle, though both are coping well. Brentford are also time wasting and doing everything possible to slow and disrupt the game. No surprise there, and the crowd's reaction is also as expected. I suspect a few beers have been taken prior to the 5:30pm kickoff, it's a good atmosphere again and we are singing constantly.

The breakthrough comes from a Ben White cross which is met brilliantly by Rice who heads home. "Sometimes you just have to put a cross in to the box" I tell Michael with authority. If he agrees he doesn't let on.

We maintain control for the rest of the half until injury time. With the stadium emptying rapidly through a combination of the pre match beers taking their toll and people's desire to top up on beer, Ramsdale takes too many touches and is charged down. The ball ends up in the net, as inevitable as the queues our departed fellow fans are now in. The ground goes silent, apart from the lower tier corner housing the Brentford fans who launch in to a chorus of "you're just a shit David Raya". Also somewhat inevitable.

As I stand to applaud the team off at the break I feel deflated, it feels like all the hard work has been undone with one mistake. There is a sense around me that Ramsdale has just underlined why Raya is first choice. This is not how anyone would want his (possibly) last game for us to go.

His fortunes change dramatically in the second half as he makes a great save at full stretch after Toney tries his luck from 45 yards. From my seat it looked in, thankfully Ramsdale just clawed it away. A free header then draws a point blank save from Ramsdale, pushing the ball over. He's definitely redeemed himself but we need to win this to really get him off the hook. Two decent penalty shouts, a third which was actually a Havertz dive (could have been a second yellow), and some near misses build the frustration and tension. Then with less than 5 minutes to go Ben White puts in another great cross and Havertz heads the winner. The noise is incredible, thoughts immediately go to Bournemouth last season, the bloke in front who I've never seen or met before turns and we high five in the melee. Michael jumps up and finds his voice. Only football can do this to people.

We see out the game in reasonable control, Arteta fist pumps the crowd. Carragher won't like that!

The A13 is kind and we get home quicker than usual, then finish the day with a couple of beers and a Chinese take away while re-watching the game on Match of the Day.

NDV: All the media focus seems to be on whether Havertz should have been sent off. Very little mention of the penalty claims or terrible time wasting and spoiler tactics Brentford employed. I saw it reported that this was the lowest percentage of ball in play time of any game in the Premier League this season, less than 50%! So much for football being part of the entertainment industry. I also see Brentford have conceded more headed goals than anyone and we have scored more headed goals than anyone. No surprise that's how both goals came, maybe we should have tried that tactic a bit more. With City and Liverpool drawing we are top of the league as we go in to the international break. But first we have the small matter of trying to turn the Porto UCL tie around.

A very tense and very late night

Tuesday 12th March 2024
UCL Porto (h) 1-0 (1-1 on agg, 4-2 on pens)

Mikel Arteta asked the fans to be loud, we didn't let him down!

I think this is the best atmosphere I've witnessed at the Emirates, possibly the UCL semi final against Man Utd started better but went flat pretty quickly after that bloke scored. And to think that was one of the last times we made it beyond the first knock out round is almost unbelievable. But we're back in the big time, reaching the quarter final for the first time since 2010, after a very hard fought tie.

I set off early, a surprisingly quick drive up meant a short wait to meet Michael then the walk to the ground. Crowds outside were light but I suspect most people were either in the pub or fighting their way through the underground after leaving work. We grabbed some dinner inside the Emirates, a very enjoyable chicken burger and chips each, washed down with a pint for the princely sum of £35.

The concourse at block 101 was filling up quickly, we took our seats about 15 minutes before kickoff and the ground was already quite full. The early playing of The Angel was much louder than the previous UCL games as a result.

The noise, and the flags and scarves waving, as the teams emerged set the scene perfectly and it seemed to help the team as they started quickly.

A couple of chances for Ødegaard and Gabriel showed our intent but, as the half wore on, we struggled to keep possession and Porto were breaking up play and wasting time as expected. To be fair they were very well organised and shut down the space around Ødegaard and Saka. Trossard, in for Martinelli, just doesn't have the pace to threaten in the same way as the young Brazilian and Michael agreed with me that we should replace him with Jesus at the break. Perhaps he heard us as he picked up a superb pass from Ødegaard and slotted home to level the tie. Cue the noise! Everyone around us, everyone in the ground it seemed, just exploded as the ball hit the net. That was followed by incredibly loud singing, more shouting actually, which I could feel rumble through me. Game on!

The second half was tense, we had chances and set pieces but Porto blocked shots and closed space out in the area better than I've seen any team do before. And they always threatened to hit, and hurt us, on the break. It was difficult not to worry about getting sucker punched as we did in the Europa League a couple of seasons ago.

The frustration grew and grew, not helped by a ridiculous refereeing performance. Trossard's twin let so many clear fouls go (by both teams) and had a peculiar way of blowing his whistle but then waiting a couple of seconds before indicating which way the free kick was being awarded. I genuinely got to the point of bewilderment rather than anger with him. Havertz escaped a booking twice, Porto were given open season to kick Saka. This was possibly the quietest I've seen Saka but with the attention he was given by the Porto players (fair and unfair) it's hardly surprising. 3 minutes of injury time would have been more like 9 or 10 in the Premier League. Extra time!

To be honest I can't remember much about the extra 30 mins. The pattern continued, Arsenal dominating possession, Porto defending well and looking for a break away. It just felt that penalties were inevitable.

And so to the shoot out. I was nervous, I said to Michael that Raya hasn't really had a stand out moment for us yet, he replied that in the Premier League we don't face any shots so how would he? Perhaps this will be his chance I said, hopefully. It was.

Ødegaard, Saka, Havertz and Rice all scored with confidence and no drama. Fair play to Saka in particular as I would probably not have selected him for the penalties. I guess that's another reason I'm in the stand and

Arteta is on the side line. Raya saved one, almost saved another and now faced the fourth Porto penalty. They needed to score to stay in the tie.

Raya picked up the ball and walked towards the taker. Mind games. The ref told him to get on his line. Raya complained the ball wasn't on the spot, it clearly was. More mind games. The lower tier of the North Bank waved their scarves and arms. The whole ground jeered, whistled and booed. The kick was taken, a split second of silence and then another explosion of noise as Raya saved brilliantly. Michael and I jumped on each other, hugging in delight. Everyone around us screaming and jumping up and down. The ground seemed to shake as the relief and unbridled joy was released after fourteen long and torturous years. We've done it!

As we composed ourselves slightly we were able to turn attention to the mass of players, subs and coaching staff on the pitch just below us jumping for joy and shouting with delight at the fans. Yes, it's only the quarter final but this means so much to everyone. The celebration police can do one, this is a moment to enjoy, to savour and to take every bit of pleasure from.

As the celebrations calmed and the players marched off to cheers and applause we stood and took in the scene. I checked my Fitbit watch, my heart rate showed I had apparently been exercising quite vigorously.

We made our way back to the car, discussing who we want in the quarter final. Anyone but City. Michael wants a big team, we settle on PSG as we haven't seen Mbappe play in person yet.

A few roadworks delay the drive home slightly so we don't get in until half past midnight. Luckily Michael has booked the morning off work so no need for the early drive to the station. Therefore there's only one way to end the day, a couple of beers watching the highlights and reliving what is probably the best time I've ever had at the Emirates.

NDV: There's been some noise about Arteta supposedly insulting the Porto manager. Arteta denies it, the other bloke has previous here as he made the same allegation against Pep and Tommy Tuchel. What happened to "what goes on the pitch, stays on the pitch"?

I spend a lot of the day watching fan clips of the last penalty and listening to podcasts about the game. The match is a bit of a blur, I think that's the tension getting in the way of the memory making part of the brain. But I do know it was a remarkable, amazing experience that I hope we are able to get much more of. Great night, now a 3 week break until the big Premier League game at City. I think I need the rest!

A point won, or a missed opportunity?

Sunday 31st March 2024
Man City (a) 0-0

Our record at the Etihad is poor but, for the first time in a very long time, we go in to this fixture with a degree of confidence that we can get something out of it. City have a few injuries (Stones, Ederson, Walker) and we are pretty much at full strength, albeit with a a couple of players carrying knocks (Saka, Zinchenko) or on their way back from longer term injuries (Jesus, Partey, Martinelli, Tomiyasu). The bench is as strong as it's been this season.

Sitting down to watch on TV, Michael opting to watch in his room, I'm not as nervous as I would normally be. Liverpool have just beaten Brighton so are clear at the top.

It turns out to be a pretty dull game, though I think you never feel that in quite the same way when it's your team playing. City come close from a corner, Jesus has a couple of chances but the keeper deals with them easily enough. It feels like one goal will be enough, neither team are playing well enough to make you think they will get it.

Pep throws on Grealish and Doku clearly deciding to push harder in attack. Arteta freshens up but largely keeps things the same in terms of tactics. Haaland finds himself unmarked at the far post and my heart sinks until he gets his feet all wrong and completely misses his kick leaving the ball to roll safely out for a goal kick.

Then our chance comes. Partey splits the City midfield with a pass to Ødegaard, he slips it perfectly out to Trossard who sprints beyond the full back. "Square it" I shout at the telly as Martinelli is free in the middle but Leo's first touch is poor and the ball holds up allowing the defender to cut off the pass option. Leo shoots rather tamely and the keeper saves comfortably. Bollocks!

The game peters out and we get a point. To be honest, neither team really deserved to win. That said, I'd have gladly accepted the three points if we had nicked them at the end. But then I would have equally gladly taken the point had it been offered before kick off.

One thing is for sure, this version of Arsenal is very much in the conversation in terms of the title.

NDV: All the stats bear out this was a top class defensive display. City had scored in their previous 57 home games, to restrict them to one shot on target (the early corner) is quite something. Will it be enough to help us win the title? Possibly not, but we have taken 4 points off each of City and Liverpool, our two main rivals. It's all to play for and we are good enough to continue the run until the end. That in itself may not be enough but this team is still young and has scope to develop further. The future is very bright.

Low key rise to the top

Wednesday 3rd April 2024
Luton Town (h) 2-0

All day I had a feeling we would win this without too much drama, confident without being cocky so to speak.

Michael had a day off and went up to London early, I drove up in double quick time - schools on Easter holidays - and got parked up. With the clocks going forward it was nice to walk to the stadium for an evening game in daylight, certainly helps when trying to avoid the copious amounts of dog shit that adorns the streets of Islington.

I met Michael whilst queuing for some food. Looking around it was noticeable that the assembled crowd on the concourse was a little more subdued than in recent games. My £16 burger, chips and beer were desperately disappointing. Stone cold chips, rock hard bun, warm burger unevenly cooked. No time to complain as kick off was fast approaching so we took our seats. Lots of new faces around, looks like people have passed/sold tickets on for this one, kind of understandable as we have a lot of big games to come in the next few weeks. And if it gives more people a chance to attend a game that has to be positive, in light of the weight of on line complaining about the ticket ballots.

The atmosphere never really got going, a few songs sprang up but didn't take a proper hold. The match reflected this in that the team seemed to settle in to a routine passing game without too many chances being created. The changes to the team certainly impacted the dynamics, without

Saka, Rice, Jorginho, Martinelli we didn't have the same oomph going forward.

The breakthrough came when Smith Rowe robbed the defender and played in to Ødegaard. He played a one two with Havertz before a beautiful first time strike gave the keeper no chance. The cheers were loud but, again, a bit subdued. It already felt like this was going to script, even more so when Smith Rowe made a great run, collected the pass from Trossard and squared the ball. Nelson appeared to have got the final touch to knock the ball over the line but the replay showed it was actually an own goal.

2-0 at the break and I wondered if we may go on and really put Luton to the sword in the second half. However, the ruthlessness we showed in recent games wasn't there tonight and the second half turned out to be more than a bit dull. It was hard not to worry that a late goal for Luton would cause some nerves but we held firm for yet another clean sheet (Raya is in pole position for the golden gloves).

At the end there was a half hearted rendition of "we are top of the league", maybe reflecting that Liverpool play Sheffield Utd tomorrow in what's likely to be an easy win.

Discussing the game afterwards with friends both at the game and who watched on tv the feeling was the same. The 3 or 4 players that came in to the starting line up just didn't match the performances of those they replaced. Yes that is understandable as they haven't played much - this was Nelson's first start in the Premier League for 4 years apparently. But it also suggests there is scope for upgrades. One for the summer.

A win, 3 points, clean sheet, top of the league. It didn't quite feel like that. Maybe a bit of fatigue creeping into the fans? There was an audible "yes" when the stadium announcer reminded the departing crowd that the next home game is Bayern in the UCL quarter final.

NDV: City won and are taking all the headlines. That may actually benefit us, it keeps the pressure off just a little. It was a decent enough performance, we were able to rest key players for bigger tests over the next few weeks and yet still got the job done.

Back on top (for now) in style

Saturday 6th April 2024
Brighton (a) 0-3

I thought this fixture was going to be a tricky one, with the danger the players could already be thinking about Tuesday night v Bayern. I needn't have worried.

I settled down to watch the game on tv, sans beer after a bit of a session with the "Croydon boys" (old work colleagues) around Richmond yesterday. Michael had buried himself in his room to watch it, reminding me of when I was living at home and would often watch games in my room, my brother doing the same in his and the old man watching in the living room. It used to drive my mum mad!

After missing good chances from Big Gabi, Saka and Jesus I was starting to get that feeling we would end up ruing the misses. Then Jesus skipped past a defender but was brought down for a penalty. A lengthy VAR check because the defender slightly brushed the ball eventually upheld the decision and Saka slotted home. Raya made a great save from a shot that was a carbon copy of the goal Porto scored against us so it remained 0-1 at the break.

A neat passing move down the right, around Saka who had been left in a heap on the floor, saw Jorginho pull the ball back from the byline and Havertz was perfectly positioned, having forced his way between two defenders, to pass it in to the net. The points were secured late on with a brilliantly taken goal from Trossard, having run 70 yards with the ball, after we broke from a Brighton corner.

The Arsenal fans behind the goal were having a great time, I had by this time succumbed to a beer. You have to celebrate the successes when they come! Back on top pending Liverpool's trip to old Trafford tomorrow, and back in some style.

NDV: Somehow Liverpool drew against Man Utd, despite having 709 shots to Utd's 2. So we are top on goal difference. It really was an impressive Arsenal win and performance on the south coast. Brighton hadn't lost at home since August, even De Zerbi described the game as finished at 2-0 because we give our opponents so few chances. Let's hope we take this form in to Tuesday night.

No bad teams at this stage

Tuesday 9th April 2024
UCL Bayern Munich (h) 2-2

There have been a lot of confident Arsenal fans on social media during the day predicting one way traffic but I am more cautious. Yes Bayern have not been their usual dominant self in the league, yes there is some discontent in the squad with Tommy Tuchel leaving at the end of the season and yes they will have no fans at the Emirates due to previous indiscretions with a few fireworks. But they have a lot of top players and going forward they can test anyone. They'll also be reeling from a loss in the league at the weekend that pretty much means the title has gone.

An ISIS threat to UCL games this week means there will be additional security checks, and the determination of the club to keep the banned Bayern fans out is likely to add to this causing inevitable delays getting into the ground, so I set off early.

Michael is at work and meeting me in the ground. As I approach the Emirates I'm a little surprised that there seem to be fewer people than usual, it's only an hour to kick off. I guess getting away from work has proved difficult for some. Another reason to be glad I retired early. There is a more visible police presence, I have to side step what the two police horses have left in the street, the smell is certainly less enticing than the pop up food tents smoky delights are emitting.

I get in to the ground after a more thorough search than is usual and head up to the upper concourse for some food. My chicken burger, chips and beer are decidedly better than last week's burger. The £16 price tag remains the same. Michael texts that he's on his way but wants a programme as a souvenir. He's been so excited for this game, the biggest game he's been to at the Emirates. I offer to find the kiosk that sells them on the upper concourse, recalling that I saw them on sale when I got my scarf a few games ago. But the ageing memory cells can't recall where the kiosk is. I set off anti clockwise in search, eventually finding it at block 120. Clockwise would have been quicker. Before I can get in the queue Michael texts to say he's already bought one. I complete my circuit and go up to our seats. There had been a real buzz downstairs, lots of loud chatter though no real singing (though that usually happens on the lower concourse). But I detect nervousness among the gooners, I'm in that camp.

Michael joins me and the build up continues with Ian Wright interviewed at pitch side - couldn't hear a bloody word of it. They really need to sort the sound system out. Then it's time for The Angel which is very loud. There's more or less a full crowd in here already; even the bloke in the row in front who ALWAYS turns up 5 minutes in to the game has got here early for this one. A fire show blasts off and then the players come out. The singing is deafening, the atmosphere is amazing. I'm shouting rather than singing, I'm not alone. Scarves are being waved, the tifos are held high, the singing seems to get even louder and I stop to take it in. The passion is pouring out of the 60,000 gooners. If there are Bayern fans secreted among us they are not evident and would do well to keep it that way.

Bayern kick off to a crescendo of boos and whistles. They're experienced at this though and it doesn't seem to affect their ability to pass the ball around. After a few minutes we start to get in to it, a Martinelli shot wide signals our intent. Then Saka fires us in front with his trademark goal, though actually Arjen Robben probably has the tm on that. The ground erupts, every part of it. It's a bit strange to see the "away section" celebrate a home goal. We have them on the back foot, Ben White gets through one on one with Neuer but hits it straight at him.

Then everything changes. A mix up between Raya and Big Gabi (Raya at fault in my view) and Gnabry is clear and equalises. Bollocks. The ground is almost silent, the balloon has been burst and the crowd find it difficult to spring back in to life. Then suddenly Sane is running at us after losing Kiwior, Saliba slides in, penalty. FFS, Kane inevitably scores. Another run through our defence is stopped at the last minute by a great Ben White tackle, 1-3 would surely have been game over. But we make it to half time trailing by just the one goal.

Michael asks me what I would change. Jorginho and Kiwior off, Rice to 6, Kai as 8/10 and Jesus up front. Zinchenko at LB.

Arteta partially agrees, swapping Zinchenko for Kiwior but that's it. We take more control but Rice is out of the game, finding no space in the tight Bayern defence. Then when they break he's 30 yards behind the play and unable to use his superpower of recovering the ball.

Trossard and Jesus finally come on, the latter changes the game with his lively running and tricky control. When he dribbles in to the area Bayern are desperately trying to block him, leaving Trossard free. Jesus fakes a shot, slips it to Leo and he levels the game. The relief and emotion explode louder than the fireworks the Bayern fans who had travelled over let off outside the ground. I'm jumping on Michael, not an easy feat as he's half a foot taller. The two young lads on my right are equally jubilant, as is everyone else in the ground.

The players don't waste time celebrating, they're keen to get on with it. We push for a winner, the crowd shouting and cheering them on. It feels like a one legged cup tie, we are desperate for the winner but they hold a threat to win it on the break. If we can't win, don't lose I exclaim. Saka collects the ball and drives in to the box, Neuer brings him down. PENALTY! is demanded from 60,000 screaming voices. The ref waves it away, the crowd are incensed. Surely VAR will give it. Surely?!

No.

The game ends, a confused ending as the ball isn't in play and Saka is still getting treatment. Then he's up and chasing the ref to plead his case. No use. It's over. 2-2.

We applaud the effort then make our way back to the car. It feels like a bad result, I've been saying for days that we need to take a lead out there. When I watch the replays I can see how the penalty wasn't given. I can't rationalise Kane not seeing red for his elbow on Big Gabi as easily. Bayern's penalty claim for what was a messed up goal kick has some merit, it feels like another sign that our defence were not in their usual groove tonight. Let's hope for better in Germany.

NDV: Still disappointed but the feeling on social media and among the pundits seems to be that we are having to learn this competition. I think there's something in that. We haven't been anywhere near our league form in the three knockout games so far but this team learns quickly. We will have to approach next week's return leg in a similar way to how we went to the Etihad. For now though, all eyes turn to Villa on Sunday.

Emery's revenge

Sunday 14th April 2024
Aston Villa (h) 0-2

After City won yesterday there was pressure on both us and Liverpool to win our respective home games to keep the title race tight.

An uneventful drive up, followed by finding a new and quicker walking route from the car to the ground, had me in good spirits. Michael had gone to the gym with Charlie so we had agreed to meet in the ground. I streamed the end of the Liverpool game on my walk and then stopped on the lower concourse to watch the last few minutes of injury time. With Palace winning 1-0 the assembled crowd were in a jovial mood, cheering every misplaced Liverpool pass, anxious looking fan on the Kop and Klopp looking increasingly angry on the side line. Songs were striking up and catching on throughout the concourse, this had the makings of a great day for us. Final whistle, Palace won. "I didn't see this coming" the bloke next to me remarked. My response was that I felt Liverpool's defeat in their Europa League first leg had probably knocked their confidence and that a similar outcome for us in the week could see us suffer the same fate next weekend at Wolves. There's that pessimism again. Unfortunately my worries were to manifest themselves much sooner.

I grabbed a beer on the upper concourse and soaked up the atmosphere. The Liverpool result had buoyed the crowd, surely it's a two horse race now, we need to win to go top and we owe Villa for the away game. I wish I could rewind to this point and find an alternative universe to play out the rest of the day.

I took my seat, no sign of Michael yet. A young bloke sat on my right, I think he's sat there before. He puffs on an e-cigarette. Yes he's been here before. The team walk on to the pitch and the noise level rises. Every player is cheered as their names are read out. The Angel is loud and passionate. We are all up for this!

And then kick off and it isn't so great. Neither team takes control, Michael still isn't here, puffy next to me is sharing his smoke with us all but luckily the wind is taking it the other way so no need for any confrontation just yet. I don't seem to be able to settle in and concentrate on the game. Finally Michael arrives, the order in Nando's was delayed. I settle in a bit more and so do Arsenal. Chances start to come our way but Saka and Jesus are both off target. Havertz is in but his finish lacks composure and confidence. Our best chance falls to Trossard but he hits it straight at the keeper.

A mix up at the back, poor communication like the other night, and Watkins is in. His shot hits the post, rolls back across the goal and somehow goes out for a goal kick. A collective sigh of relief echos around the North Bank.

Half time, hopefully Arteta will reorganise and gee them up a bit. We need to win this.

But the second half was poor. Villa sat deep, constricted space and denied us the opportunity to create anything of real note. It felt very similar to Bayern, but this time we had no answer. Changes felt essential but were slow in coming. Jesus off and Havertz back up front, Zinchenko off and Jorginho on to bring some control. It just made no difference. Smith Rowe for Ødegaard seemed a bit odd, apparently a slight injury I later found out (worrying for the upcoming Bayern game).

Villa had a series of threatening corners, we just couldn't clear it or get decent possession. The crowd become increasingly agitated, I realise I'm not joining in the singing as my nerves are increasing. Then a cross, everyone misses it but Bailey at the far post, unmarked, finishes well. The ground is silent except for the large Villa contingent who go bananas. It generates a response from our fans, a quick burst of song, I join in.

As we try to push forward to get an equaliser Villa break, Watkins shakes of Smith Rowe and scores. The ground immediately starts to empty. A bloke several rows behind us takes umbrage and shouts at the departing fans. One turns to remonstrate and for a few seconds it looks like a fist fight is about to break out. How can it turn so sour so quickly?

Full time and Emi Martinez milks the win with the Villa fans, you can't blame him I suppose.

We make our way home but have to walk among the jubilant away fans. Thankfully their songs are not too insulting and a small police presence is enough to stop any unpleasantness breaking out.

The car journey is quiet, I put an 80s music station on rather than listen to City fans babbling on about the double treble. Match of the Day 2 is deleted immediately from the Sky box and I watch The Sweeney to wash away the events of the day. I hate football.

NDV: I haven't looked at social media or the stats but my overriding feeling is one of missed opportunity. It feels like the period after Christmas where we had a blip, but this time there is no Dubai trip to reset and recharge the players. Arteta spoke about Wednesday being a "beautiful chance" to respond. We are going to need a stand out performance to beat Bayern out there. Is this team capable of such? Definitely, but attitude, tactics and belief are going to need to be much better than we showed against Villa. COYG!

Running out of steam!

Wednesday 17th April 2024
UCL Bayern Munich (a) 1-0

I sat down to watch this on tv with pretty low confidence. Bayern have been poor by their standards this season and had several key players out injured or suspended. But this is now their last chance to win something after Leverkusen secured the Bundesliga title last weekend. Big up to Grant Xhaka.

We started confidently enough, passing the ball without threatening too much. Bayern responded well, forced a couple of saves from Raya and came close to opening the scoring but it was Arsenal who ended the half in the ascendency.

Then for the first 15 minutes of the second half we took the game to them, forcing turnovers. But, as with the first leg, we failed to capitalise while on top. The Bayern goal, when it inevitably came, was simply poor defending on our part, allowing Kimmich to steal in and head a cross home. Too many static defenders watching him.

Changes came, Jesus and Trossard on, but it made little difference unfortunately. It was eerily similar to the Villa game, we ran out of ideas and ran out of puff (perhaps we should get that young bloke who sat next to me in the team).

The final act of the game summed it up. A corner. "It's now or never time" the tv commentator said. He was spot on. Saka wasn't, his corner failed to beat the first man and the referee blew to end our UCL journey for this season.

NDV: At the start of the season I thought the quarter final was the minimum we should achieve and felt, if the draw was kind, that a semi final or better was possible. I was adamant we needed to take a lead to Munich as their home form in this competition is top notch. On the night it was clear we needed to score first if we were going to progress. In the end our inexperience was a key factor, game management in both legs not at the level required. But this is a young team and they will improve. I'm less frustrated with this than I was with the Villa game, and it's the Premier League we must now step up in. There are six games left, we need to win the next two (both before City play again), put a 4 point lead on the board and, most importantly, put some pressure on them. What we must not do is stumble towards the end of the season in the way we did last year.

Superb on the road

Saturday 20th April 2024
Wolves (a) 0-2

An unusual Saturday evening kick off time puts paid to our normal movie night which Mary, as understanding and reasonable as ever, is prepared to forgo in the interest of a title challenge. She's watching "strictly come jungle on ice", or something along those lines, while I try to calm my pre match nerves with a cold beer or two. Wolves have been a bit up and down this season but it's worth remembering they beat City at Molineux, so shouldn't be underestimated.

We started well, carving out chances but not finishing particularly well. We seem to have dropped off a bit in that regard in the last few games. With no goals in our last two, this is not the time to make that a hat trick.

The best chance then fell to Wolves after a mistake at the back left the striker bearing down on goal. His shot from a tight angle was on target but Raya did well to push it on to the post before it was cleared. Rice picked up a booking for committing a foul to stop the game when Havertz was down injured. I'm not a believer in referees stopping the game when a player is down, unless it's a head injury of course, so had no issue with him playing on, or with Rice's decision to take one for the team. But, when you see the challenge that left Havertz rolling in pain, it's surely as clear a red card as you could ever wish to see. Nope. VAR happily cleared the challenge. Honestly, what's the point in VAR if it is going to allow horrendous, potentially dangerous challenges like that to go unpunished. The primary responsibility of match officials is to ensure the safety of the players, it's hard to square that with this decision.

Arsenal responded in the best possible way, a cheeky toe poke strike from Trossard in to the top corner on the stroke of half time. Get in you beauty!

We took the game to Wolves second half. The defence solid, the midfield in complete control, the attack threatening. Havertz had a good effort saved before a late attack ended with Ødegaard on the edge of the six yard box. His cut back was blocked but, when the ball rebounded to him, he squeezed his shot in at the near post for 2-0. Game over, three points and we march on.

NDV: This was another fantastic away day performance and result. Defensively, we are so strong away from home, keeping clean sheet after clean sheet. Best defence in the Premier League. I'm always nervous watching games where it's close in terms of the score (you may have noticed that) but, yet again, the stats show this was a dominant performance, 24 shots to their 5. This young team just seems to be getting better and better.

On cloud nine (literally)

Tuesday 23rd April 2024
Chelsea (h) 5-0

I thought I had learned my lesson about booking holidays mid season after missing the Spurs and UCL games in September. So I researched the fixtures carefully before booking a couple of days away with Mary in Riga. The plan was to meet Mary's brother Teague (another massive Arsenal fan) and his wife Nijole, though that didn't materialise as they had to cancel last minute. When I checked the fixtures this was a free week and the Chelsea match had already been moved for tv to an early kick off on March 16th. Then Chelsea made it through in the FA Cup so the league game was moved. I frantically tried to move the flights so I could go to the game or, at worst, watch it on tv. That wasn't possible so I had to endure being in the air while the game was on. Gutted doesn't begin to cover it.

As we took off I learned British Airways was providing "messaging Wi-Fi" on the flight for free, or you could pay to stream. I knew the streaming wouldn't work but used the free option to keep in touch with what was happening on the ground.

I text Michael but, as his battery was low, he was unable to respond. Luckily two mates, Mark (big Chelsea fan) and Paul (big Arsenal fan), were able to keep me posted. I've talked before about how football fans are often pessimistic about their own team and this was very evident in the tone of my two aspiring football correspondent pals.

Mark bemoaned the early Arsenal goal and declared the game over at 1-0. A couple of missed Chelsea chances confirming his belief. Paul was deeply concerned that we missed chances in the first half to make it 2-0 and was convinced we would live to regret it. Until, that is, we made it 2-0 and both he watching on tv at home and me, hanging on his every word update, breathed a collective sigh of relief and enjoyed life as goals 3, 4 and 5 went in.

Having made it home in the small hours I set about finding the highlights and savouring the win. More than a tinge of regret for missing the game but at least my seat wasn't empty as Charlie accompanied Michael. They both had a wonderful time, Michael off to work the next day with a smile as I dropped him at the station.

NDV: This was a stunningly good performance in which we recorded our biggest ever win against Chelsea. All the stats show how dominant we were. I'm just annoyed at missing it - "bad planning on your part" my less than sympathetic son reflected. I'm particularly disappointed I missed the Arsenal fans sarcastically shouting "ole" near the end as Chelsea managed to string a few passes together.

Derby Day Delight

Sunday 28th April 2024
Tottenham (a) 2-3

A very late night, (or is it early morning when you go to bed at 6am?) after friends Kev and Kim came over for an overdue get together, may not be the best preparation for such a big game, even if only watching on tv. Kev is a lifelong Chelsea fan so had to endure a bit of stick over the midweek result, Michael chipping in with me suitably.

When I woke at 1pm the team news had just come out and happily it was an unchanged eleven and with no obvious injury news.

This season I have found it very difficult and immensely stressful watching the big games on tv. My watch told me my heart rate was up significantly and we had only played two minutes. An OG from a Saka corner relaxed me a little but that was undone when Spurs appeared to equalise. For once VAR came to our rescue ruling the goal offside by the tightest of margins. Phew!

Then two shouts for a penalty from Spurs, both waved away, before Saka cleared to Havertz. He held on to the ball and played a superb pass back to Saka who roasted the defender and slotted home in his trademark fashion. I'm not giving Robben any credit now, that's a Saka style goal. I celebrated hesitantly though as I was convinced VAR would pull it back and award them a penalty. Somewhat surprisingly they didn't. 2-0.

A third goal beautifully headed home by Havertz from a corner drew very loud cheers from me and Michael, upstairs in his room. Rice's delivery was perfect despite the abuse he was getting from three of the most unfortunate looking Spurs fans in the crowd. Rice immediately turned to give them some stick, similar to what Saka did after the first two goals, resulting in them turning around and leaving the scene with their tails between their legs. Oh I do love the derby.

We had complete control in the second half and I was having to stop myself pondering another 5-0 win and calculating the effect it could have on our goal difference. Then Raya had a brain fart, gifting them a goal. The mood in the stadium and in the living room took a desperate turn for the worse.

When they were given a penalty (correctly) despite being denied initially, I knew it was going in. I'll be honest, at this point I was convinced they would equalise and our title tilt would end. I haven't felt so stressed and uncomfortable watching a game since the 2017 FA Cup Final when we beat Chelsea to deny them the double, Per and Holding performing heroics to hold on to the win.

The relief when the final whistle went was incredible. And that was pretty much the only emotion, definitely lacking the usual euphoria a derby win brings. This is a different Arsenal now, the character and belief that was so clearly missing in previous seasons now so evident in, what is still, a very young team. The tv analysis afterwards seemed, to me at least, to focus more on how we nearly messed up rather than how we stood firm when the game changed. Paul Merson having a dig at Gavin's (from Gavin and Stacey) "favourite Spurs player" Michael Dawson was very funny though.

NDV: I spent last night and this morning trawling social media for any and all video I could find from the game. Some belters from the Spurs end showing Saka and Rice giving them stick. My lasting impression though is one of much less jubilation than I would normally expect after a win at their place. I'm not sure if it's the tense finish, the overwhelming feeling of relief that we didn't totally mess it up or the fact City inevitably strolled to a victory at Forest. Whatever the reason, the fact remains we are still top, they can overtake us if they win the game in hand and we have to just keep winning to keep the pressure up. Whatever happens from here it will have been a remarkable season so I'm going to try and enjoy the remaining games as best I can.

Taking it to the wire!

Saturday 4th May 2024
Bournemouth (h) 3-0

An early start for the 12:30 kick off and we're on the train so we can enjoy a beer in the sunshine later. Michael went up separately as he had an errand to run first. I was on a mission to get in the stadium early and take photos to be used for the book cover illustration. I had a lovely chat this week with a fantastic artist, Ruth Beck, who has kindly agreed to paint a picture that will form the front cover. So I'm really excited and determined to get the photo just right. You can judge the final outcome for yourselves.

Photos taken, I nip back down to the concourse at block 101 and get some much needed breakfast. Whilst enjoying my gourmet sausage and pint of lager I get talking to a young fella who tells me about his nightmare journey to Baku for the Europa League final against Chelsea. It reaffirms my reluctance to travel for big European games, even if I could get a ticket. That said, if we make a Champions League final I'd love to go.

Michael arrives and I duly hand him the pint I bought him, telling him "that's first class service". We discuss team news, unchanged again with a strong bench.

We take our seats and the teams emerge from the tunnel into the bright sunlight, flags waving, tifo on display and flames bursting from the "fire boxes". I don't know what they are called so settled on that name.

The Angel is sung loudly by the almost full stadium, everyone seems to be up for this game. Perhaps it's the memory of last season's dramatic, last gasp win coupled with the need to take all three points today. Real pressure, real jeopardy.

We start well and put Bournemouth under a lot of pressure. A couple of early chances spurned but I feel supremely confident that we are going to win this. Most unlike me, perhaps the beer helps with the nerves - it used to work for snooker player Bill Werbeniuk (Google it).

As we reach the fourteenth minute everyone stands and applauds as a touching tribute to Daniel Anjorin, the innocent 14 year old Arsenal fan murdered on his way to school this week. What is this country coming to?

I say everyone stands, actually there were two women, a couple of rows in front, who remained seated, apparently oblivious to what was going on, while tapping away on their phones. Again, what is this country coming to?

Arsenal continue to threaten but also continue to miss chances. A goal would round off what has been one of the best halves we have played all season. Just before the break, we get one. Havertz is fouled by the keeper, a VAR check goes on for about three hours and eventually it's confirmed. Saka strokes the ball home with the utmost confidence and it's 1-0.

We meet Charlie for a pint at half time, the beer is slipping down a little too easily today.

Bournemouth are much better in the second half and push forward. We escape an equaliser after a foul on Raya. It looked pretty clear from my seat, though it was at the Clock End so quite a distance for my old eyes. This is underlined when I mistake Saliba for White. Michael responds with typical concern and compassion for his Dad. Not!

A good attacking move finds Rice sprinting in to the box, he adjusts brilliantly to square the ball to Trossard who beats the keeper with a powerful shot. The new "Trossard again, ole, ole" song rings out and the points are surely safe now. There are smiles everywhere and the singing picks up in celebration.

Then in injury time Rice picks up a "no look" pass from Jesus, takes a touch to control it and fires home for 3-0.

"We are top of the league" rings out as the game comes to an end. We may not win it but this season we are pushing City all the way to the end.

A cheeky beer on the way to the station rounds off a brilliant day. Whatever the outcome this season, it's days like these that make the season ticket worthwhile. A sunny day, great atmosphere, a few beers with my son (and his mate) and excellent, elite level football. We are very lucky we are able to do this when so many others will not get that opportunity. Especially poor Daniel Anjorin, may he rest in peace.

NDV: There has been a lot of noise about the penalty being harsh and the disallowed Bournemouth goal being very fortunate for Arsenal. Whilst I agree the decisions did favour us I would point out they got away with a blatant red card challenge on Saka. Weirdly, that isn't getting any airtime. I'd also point out that in the stadium it seemed that the penalty and disallowed goal were no brainers, so perhaps this should be considered in terms of the communication fans get, or more to the point, don't get.

They think it's all over, but not yet!

Sunday 12th May 2024
Man Utd (a) 0-1

After City won at Fulham their fans celebrated with an air of the title race having been won. Likewise, a lot of online comments from Arsenal fans (sensible ones and not so sensible ones) appear to have given up hope. I lived through the 1989 league run in so will never accept it's over until it is mathematically impossible for us to win it, but I will admit it does look like City are in that groove that will see them win their remaining games. It's out of our hands, all we can do is win our last two games.

As I sit down to watch us at OT I'm not feeling very confident. We have a poor record up there, if we are to push the title race to the last weekend, we need a rare win. When the teams are announced it's hard to be pessimistic though, we are unchanged while they are playing an injury hit team with Casemiro in defence. He was awful against Palace. But, always the pessimist, I can't help thinking of 2016 and the surprise defeat to the very depleted Utd team. We had just beaten Leicester and were looking good to go on and win the league, but the OT curse struck again.

The game kicks off and, almost immediately, something happens that kind of puts football and the title race in to perspective. Mary has been off work with a pretty nasty chest infection. She has a severe coughing fit and is struggling to breathe. The football can wait. Thankfully she recovers and is ok, I rejoin the match with about ten minutes gone.

It's hard to concentrate on the game and, even when Trossard (again, ole, ole) scores, I don't feel the usual elation. A weak "yeah" comes out but my mind isn't really on the game.

I settle in a bit more than the Arsenal do, we aren't giving up chances but we look a bit slow and ponderous. That said, we have a couple of chances which are both wide from Ben White. Michael comes in from his mate's house and dashes upstairs to watch the game on the tv in his room. Utd are growing in confidence so the half time whistle is very welcome.

I check on the patient and, thankfully, she's ok. Big second half required from the Arsenal, an early goal to double the lead would be nice.

The goal doesn't come, we just don't look as composed and confident as we have done recently. United gradually grow in to the game but their decision making in the final third is poor and Raya isn't particularly troubled. Then Arsenal push up and take the game to them a bit more. With twenty minutes to go I'm getting more and more nervous. As the clock ticks down to ten minutes left we start to get on top. A couple of wasted corners and a weak Ødegaard shot show intent, we then draw a couple of saves from the keeper and my nerves are settling. Saka comes off injured and is replaced by Jesus. He doesn't really get in to the game but as we go in to injury time we are holding firm. After so many impressive away performances this season I think it's understandable we sit deep and back ourselves to keep a clean sheet. But, as a fan, it's not easy watching.

When the final whistle came the main feeling I had was relief. Whatever happens from here we have taken it to the final game of the season. This is a big step up from last year, though relying on Spurs or the Hammers to do us a favour doesn't fill me with confidence that we will end up Champions. But you never know...

NDV: Usually, after a win against one of our main rivals, I would feel elation and excitement. For some reason, today is a bit different. Whether it's the below par performance, or City's stroll to victory, I'm not sure but the narrative of the online discourse is one of (almost) resignation that we will come up short in the title race. The stats from yesterday bear out the feeling that we didn't really perform to the level we have seen recently but, as many are reflecting, at this stage of the season it's entirely about results. Get the points, that's all that matters. We have pushed the title race to the last game, whatever happens between Spurs and City. I'm now swapping texts with Michael to plan our final match day. A spot of pre match lunch and a few beers will be the order of the day. If the dream materialises it could turn in to a very late night, and it will probably get messy!

It wasn't to be

Sunday 19th May 2024
Everton (h) 2-1

I wanted to see us maintain a title challenge right to the end this season, to show we have progressed. We have done exactly that. We always make a big day out of the last home game, this is going to be even bigger than usual. We set off early by train and meet Charlie, his Dad Gary and friends Jason and Rebecca for an early lunch. As we walk out of the underground station the brightness and warmth of the sun really hit. Holloway Road is already bustling with people, the vast majority wearing Arsenal shirts. People are sitting outside cafes eating and drinking, there's already a party feel to the day.

As we eat lunch, and sip a beer or two, I keep an eye on the Horatia pub opposite. There are already quite a few people on the pavement outside enjoying the weather and building up to the big game with a few beers. We head over to join them.

There's a brilliant atmosphere among the fans, songs break out sporadically and there is a lot of laughter. The brass band that the club have engaged to add to today's festivities marches along Holloway Road and stops on the corner by the pub. I can't see them because of the sea of arms held aloft with phones capturing the moment but I can certainly hear them. We all join in with the singing, this is such a brilliant day.

We head to the stadium, there's a big crowd gathered by the club shop, the Armoury. Some are in the long queue to buy the new home shirt but most are just enjoying the band who are now playing at the foot of the stairs. It seems to me that everyone is determined to enjoy the day, it's great to see so many people having a good time together with the common bond that is the Arsenal.

We meet up inside, having decided not to test the theory that you can enter any turnstile rather than your designated one. I get talking to a couple of young lads from the USA, Iowa to be exact. We watch as the Ashburton Army march reaches the stadium and I explain to the two lads what is going on. After another beer we walk in to Block 101 for the final time this season, I bump in to my mate Stuart. Mary and I were due to be out yesterday with Stu and his wife Karen, old neighbours who are still good friends, but Mary is still suffering with the chest infection so we had to cancel.

Climbing the stairs to our seat I feel a little sad that this will be the last one for a while. But the packed stand is full of excited, expectant fans smiling and laughing and eager for the game to start, so my mood soon brightens.

The teams emerge and the noise is deafening. Everton decide to switch ends, not a popular decision, and a chorus of boos rings out. The Angel starts and I honestly think every single person is joining in, I rate this the best rendition of the season.

Arsenal start well, Martinelli is put through and forces a good save from the keeper. The crowd are buzzing, the ground is rocking. Could this turn out how we hope? Then it all goes flat as news of a City goal permeates the stadium. Songs start again as we are determined not to go down without a fight, but it seems the players are aware of events in Manchester. You can see a slight slump in their shoulders, but as professionals they continue their efforts to find a goal. Everton hit the post and then the side netting. The away fans think it's in, but thankfully not. The game drifts a bit, a City second goal has changed the atmosphere completely. There's now a resignation that it's over. A deflected Everton goal draws even more life out of the crowd. As much as I had expected City to win it the reality is still hard to take. Then suddenly there's a murmur around us, West Ham have pulled a goal back. The cheers spread around the ground, maybe it's back on? I don't know if the players picked up on this but either way they are not giving up just yet. Ødegaard pulls the ball back from deep and in comes Tomi to fire home the equaliser through a crowd of defenders. Muscle memory kicks in, we all stand and celebrate the goal, a defiance is suddenly evident. Half time.

I can't remember the exact order of events in the second half. Raya made a great save, Havertz hit the post. City scored a third, West Ham apparently pulled one back but then that was ruled out by VAR. We sang some songs and I chatted to the two young lads beside me. We created chances, the keeper made a good save, Smith Rowe hit the post but a winning goal was looking unlikely despite the desire for one shared by the fans and players alike. As the game appeared to be drifting to an unsatisfactory conclusion Jesus nicked the ball in the Everton half and put Ødegaard in. He slid the ball to Havertz who tucked it away. Get in. We end with a win. But hang on, VAR! When the referee was sent to the screen you just knew he would rule the goal out. But no! He awards the goal and we celebrate again. Full time, season over. We end with a hard fought win and another three points to take the total to 89, the second highest the club has ever achieved. Only the Invincibles bettered it, and only by one point.

We stayed behind, like most of the ground, to applaud the players on their lap of appreciation and to hear the captain and manager speak. The sound system wasn't great but you could see both were incredibly disappointed but also determined to go again next season. Michael insisted we have one more beer before we go, I didn't need much persuading. We'll be back in August and do it all again. Hopefully this time next year we are celebrating a different outcome.

NDV: I avoided social media and didn't watch Match of the Day. I just didn't want to see any of it. Despite the outcome I really enjoyed the day. We have been on great form lately and this win felt like the ending we needed. There was a weird sense of relief, weird because ultimately this result had no impact on the league table. But I think it was important to win for the mindset of players and fans alike. It completed a run of six consecutive league wins in the run in to the end of the season. This is what we had hoped for, a run in where we were imperious. Unfortunately, the starting point for those six games had City ahead. But we have shown this team isn't finished, it's only just getting started.

Continuing to be an Arsenal Supporter

Where does the team go from here?

Despite the disappointing end to this season there is certainly much optimism for the club in the coming years. The squad is still one of the youngest in the Premier League but has already gained invaluable experience in challenging for the title and competing in Europe.

With anticipated new signings in the summer of 2024, there will be high expectations that Mikel Arteta's squad will once again mount a serious challenge for the Premier League and, hopefully, in the Champions League and domestic cup competitions.

The standard required to win the Premier League has never been higher. The team that clinches the title next May will probably have to acquire 90+ points, that would be a new club record for Arsenal. This season we lost five games (Fulham, Villa x2, West Ham, Newcastle), that's too many really and, certainly, an area where the team needs to improve. Turning two of those in to draws would have been enough to win the league on goal difference but, to be fair, the margins in several of those games were so fine it would be churlish to criticise too much.

But then, as Arteta himself said on the last day, we shouldnt settle for what we have achieved so far. The club is full of winners and that is the mentality that will be needed to get us over the line and win the big trophies.

I'm confident Arsenal will continue to develop and grow in to a force for many years to come. Hopefully that delivers trophies but, either way, we will be supporting them throughout the journey.

What's next for the Fox boys?

With so much to look forward to we have no intention of giving up the season tickets any time soon, even if getting to games becomes more difficult for me. The ability to pass tickets on to friends and family via the ticket exchange, and the option to sell individual game tickets makes long term retention viable. Sorry if you are on the waiting list hoping for fewer people to renew each year. Your time will come eventually.

I'd love to travel to see Arsenal in a big UCL away game, Juventus would be my first choice as Michael and I haven't been there yet. But any of the top teams, preferably in a semi final, would be a brilliant experience.

Whatever the future holds for this amazing group of players, and the ones that follow them, you can be sure we will be there supporting them as often as possible, in Block 101, Row 25.

If you are in the area for a home game, stop by and say hello. You can't miss us, I'll be the old boy singing out of tune (and probably a bit pissed). Michael will be the lovable big lump who's always beside me.

THE END - but only for this season!

Glossary of terms

Gooners - nickname for Arsenal fans

COYG - Come On You Gunners! A rallying call the Arsenal fans shout

UCL - UEFA Champions League, UEFA's premier competition pitting the best sides against each other to earn the right to be European Champions

EPL - English Premier League

FAC - Football Association (FA) Cup. The oldest and probably still the most prestigious cup competition in the world. Arsenal have won it more than any other club

EFL Cup - English Football League Cup, second order domestic cup competition

VAR - Video Assistant Referee, designed to aid the on field officials by spotting errors and confirming marginal decisions. Horrendously inconsistent application has many fans questioning continued use

TFL - Transport for London, transport authority for the capital

Arsecast - Podcast on all things Arsenal presented by Andrew Mangan (otherwise known as Arseblog). Top quality entertainment

Arsenal Vision - Another top quality Arsenal based podcast hosted by Elliot Smith (block him on Twitter/X) who predicts Arsenal will win every game 10-0

Bollocks - English expression meaning "oh dear, things are not working out as one had hoped", or talking nonsense

Sky - Sky Sports tv company who own Premier League rights in the UK

TNT - Similar to Sky, responsible for 1230pm kick off on a Saturday

OT - Old Trafford, home of Man Utd where Arsenal clinched 2001/02 title

About the author

David Fox was born in the City of London Maternity Hospital in Islington, North London. As the, long since closed, hospital was only a mile from where the Emirates Stadium now stands, and close enough to be covered by modern day match day parking restrictions, he was probably always destined to become an Arsenal fan.

Growing up on the Finsbury Estate, near Smithfield meat market, he spent most of his time playing, and developing a love of, football with older brother, Simon, and a host of other estate kids. As one of the youngest kids in the bunch he was always shoved in goal but used this to develop skills that saw him represent both junior and secondary school in that position.

After leaving school he had a brief career in the Civil Service, where he met wife Mary, before moving on to BT and the burgeoning 1980s IT industry. After they were married, David and Mary moved to Essex and had two children, Nicola and Michael.

After a successful thirty year career with BT, David took early retirement and now spends most of his time either completing DIY projects, planning and taking holidays or exercising while listening to, predominantly, Arsenal based podcasts.

When Mary retires, they plan to relocate to more a rural and tranquil setting and David intends to continue writing. Whatever the future brings, Arsenal will always be a major part of David's life.

Printed in Great Britain
by Amazon